SAGE was founded in 1965 by Sara Miller McCune to support the dissemination of usable knowledge by publishing innovative and high-quality research and teaching content. Today, we publish over 900 journals, including those of more than 400 learned societies, more than 800 new books per year, and a growing range of library products including archives, data, case studies, reports, and video. SAGE remains majority-owned by our founder, and after Sara's lifetime will become owned by a charitable trust that secures our continued independence.

Los Angeles | London | New Delhi | Singapore | Washington DC | Melbourne

INFRASTRUCTURE

PPP AND LAW

FOR EXECUTIVES

ANURAG K. AGARWAL

INFRASTRUCTURE PPP AND LAW FOR EXECUTIVES

$SAGE

Los Angeles | London | New Delhi
Singapore | Washington DC | Melbourne

Copyright © Anurag K. Agarwal, 2019

All rights reserved. No part of this book may be reproduced or utilized in any form or by any means, electronic or mechanical, including photocopying, recording or by any information storage or retrieval system, without permission in writing from the publisher.

First published in 2019 by

SAGE Publications India Pvt Ltd
B1/I-1 Mohan Cooperative Industrial Area
Mathura Road, New Delhi 110 044, India
www.sagepub.in

SAGE Publications Inc
2455 Teller Road
Thousand Oaks, California 91320, USA

SAGE Publications Ltd
1 Oliver's Yard, 55 City Road
London EC1Y 1SP, United Kingdom

SAGE Publications Asia-Pacific Pte Ltd
18 Cross Street #10-10/11/12
China Square Central
Singapore 048423

Published by Vivek Mehra for SAGE Publications India Pvt Ltd. Typeset in 11/14.5 pt Sabon by Fidus Design Pvt Ltd, Chandigarh.

Library of Congress Cataloging-in-Publication Data Available

ISBN: 978-93-532-8683-5 (PB)

SAGE Team: Namarita Kathait, Manisha Mathews, Shruti Gupta, Madhurima Thapa and Rajinder Kaur

Dedicated to

Babuji

Late Shri Krishna Bahadur Sinha,
Senior Advocate

An institution in himself

Thank you for choosing a SAGE product!
If you have any comment, observation or feedback,
I would like to personally hear from you.

Please write to me at **contactceo@sagepub.in**

Vivek Mehra, Managing Director and CEO, SAGE India.

Bulk Sales

SAGE India offers special discounts
for purchase of books in bulk.
We also make available special imprints
and excerpts from our books on demand.

For orders and enquiries, write to us at

Marketing Department
SAGE Publications India Pvt Ltd
B1/I-1, Mohan Cooperative Industrial Area
Mathura Road, Post Bag 7
New Delhi 110044, India

E-mail us at **marketing@sagepub.in**

Subscribe to our mailing list

Write to **marketing@sagepub.in**

This book is also available as an e-book.

CONTENTS

List of Abbreviations ix
Preface xiii

1 Introduction 1
2 Sectoral Laws and Regulations 23
3 Laws and Regulations across Sectors 87
4 Challenges to Infrastructure Development in India 109
5 Funding and Legal Framework 127
6 Judiciary and Infrastructure 149
7 Political Will and Intention 173

Appendix: Important Terms Related to Infrastructure Projects 199
About the Author 205

LIST OF ABBREVIATIONS

AAI	Airports Authority of India
AAP	Aam Aadmi Party
AERA	Airports Economic Regulatory Authority
APTEL	Appellate Tribunal for Electricity
ARR	Annual Revenue Requirement
BLT	Build–lease–transfer
BMIC	Bengaluru–Mysuru Infrastructure Corridor
BOLT	Build–own–lease–transfer
BOO	Build–own–operate
BOOT	Build–own–operate–transfer
BOT	Build–operate–transfer
CA	Concession agreement
CAG	Comptroller and Auditor General of India
CCI	Competition Commission of India
CCTV	Closed-circuit television
CEA	Central Electricity Authority
CERC	Central Electricity Regulatory Commission
CoC	Committee of Creditors
COD	Commercial operation date
CoS	Committee of Secretaries
CPCB	Central Pollution Control Board
CSIA	Chhatrapati Shivaji International Airport
DB	Design–build
DBF	Design–build–finance
DBFM	Design–build–finance–maintain
DBFO	Design–build–finance–operate
DBFOM	Design–build–finance–operate–maintain

DBFOT		Design–build–finance–operate–transfer
DBO		Design–build–operate
DGCA		Directorate General of Civil Aviation
DGS&D		Directorate General of Supplies and Disposals
DIAL		Delhi International Airport Limited
DIFC		Dubai International Financial Centre
DMIC		Delhi–Mumbai Industrial Corridor Project
DTH		Direct-to-Home
EGoM		Empowered Group of Ministers
EOI		Expression of interest
EPC		Engineering, Procurement and Construction
GEC		Guaranteed energy consumption
GeM		Government eMarketplace
GIDA		Gujarat Infrastructure Development Act
GIDB		Gujarat Infrastructure Development Board
GIDC		Gujarat Industrial Development Corporation
GIFT		Gujarat International Finance Tec-City
GoI		Government of India
GoM		Group of Ministers
GUDC		Gujarat Urban Development Corporation
GUVNL		Gujarat Urja Vikas Nigam Limited
HAM		Hybrid annuity model
HPEC		High Powered Expert Committee
HR		Hyundai Rotem
IBBI		Insolvency and Bankruptcy Board of India
IBC		Insolvency and Bankruptcy Code
ICP		Integrated check post
IE		Independent engineer
ILFC		International Lease Finance Corporation
IL&FS		Infrastructure Leasing & Financial Services
IMG		Inter-ministerial group
IRDA		Insurance Regulatory and Development Authority
IRP		Interim resolution professional

IRSDC	Indian Railway Stations Development Corporation
IT	Information technology
JICA	Japan International Cooperation Agency
JV	Joint venture
LPAI	Land Ports Authority of India
MCA	Model Concession Agreement
MIAL	Mumbai International Airport Limited
MoU	Memorandum of understanding
MTA	Massachusetts Turnpike Authority
NCLT	National Company Law Tribunal
NCLAT	National Company Law Appellate Tribunal
NCR	National Capital Region
NDA	National Democratic Alliance
NGT	National Green Tribunal
NHAI	National Highways Authority of India
NICE	Nandi Infrastructure Corridor Enterprise
NPA	Non-performing asset
OECD	Organisation for Economic Co-operation and Development
OMDA	Operation, Management and Development Agreement
PIL	Public Interest Litigation
POG	Procurement of goods
PPA	Power purchase agreement
PPP	Public–private partnership
PSU	Public sector undertaking
PWD	Public Works Department
R&R	Rehabilitation and Resettlement
RBI	Reserve Bank of India
RFCTLARR Act	Right to Fair Compensation and Transparency in Land Acquisition, Rehabilitation and Resettlement Act

RfP	Request for proposal
RfQ	Request for qualification
RoFR	Right of first refusal
ROI	Return on investment
ROT	Rehabilitate–operate–transfer
SAROD	Society for Affordable Redressal of Disputes
SCM	Smart Cities Mission
SEBI	Securities and Exchange Board of India
SERC	State Electricity Regulatory Commission
SEZ	Special economic zone
SHA	Shareholders agreement
SIPE	Supply and installation of plant and equipment
SIR	Special Investment Region
SLP	Special Leave Petition
SPV	Special purpose vehicle
SSA	State Support Agreement
T&D	Transmission and distribution
TAMP	Tariff Authority for Major Ports
TDSAT	Telecom Disputes Settlement and Appellate Tribunal
TNPCB	Tamil Nadu Pollution Control Board
TPC	Total project cost
TRAI	Telecom Regulatory Authority of India
UMPP	Ultra Mega Power Project
UoI	Union of India
UPA	United Progressive Alliance
VHB	Vanasse Hangen Brustlin, Inc.
VIP	Very important person

PREFACE

I dedicate this book to Babuji, Late Shri Krishna Bahadur Sinha, Senior Advocate. I had the good fortune of attending his chambers at Lucknow when my father, Late Shri Ram Lakhan Agarwal, Advocate, sent me to Babuji, his senior colleague in the profession, immediately after my final law examinations. Babuji was an institution in himself—profound knowledge of the law; unflinching traits of integrity, dedication, sincerity and confidence; fastidious in appearance; meticulous in preparation; unique blend of a hard taskmaster and passionate individual and, above all, a fatherly figure for all his juniors. The environment of his chambers was like that of a *gurukul* (an institution where students are like a part of the teacher's family) and facilitated learning the finer aspects of the legal practice, besides instilling camaraderie and character building.

According to recent reports of the World Bank regarding public–private partnership (PPP) and infrastructure in India, there had been a slowdown in PPPs in India during the first half of 2010, which was quite opposite to what was the situation in the country in the early 2000s, and once again in the second half of 2010, the PPP growth story has taken an upward trend. There has been a new wave of confidence and trust in the Indian infrastructure sector with foreign and domestic investors preferring to show willingness to invest in long-term projects and wait patiently for return on investment (ROI). This is a major change and in this positive business environment about PPPs and infrastructure, certain major challenges being faced by the infrastructure companies are primarily legal and regulatory.

There couldn't have been a better time for publishing a book like this, which is immensely needed by the business executives to understand the legal and regulatory nuances in simple language, without using jargon and without being highly technical. Though the book is written in easy-to-understand language, there is enough rigour so as to get a good insight into the legal and regulatory issues in PPPs and infrastructure. Numerous cases have been discussed in all the chapters of the book so that the reader gets proper exposure to the practical situations and the realistic nature of issues in different sectors of infrastructure in India. The role of politics and government, especially in a democratic country like India, has also been highlighted.

The book is divided into seven chapters. The first chapter—'Introduction'—talks about the importance of proper infrastructure for modern living and how PPP has become important for creating the required infrastructural set-up in India. There is emphasis on the point that it is not possible for the government alone to take care of all the infrastructural needs of the society, and hence, private participation is necessary to fulfil the dreams of the teeming millions in the country. The second chapter—'Sectoral Laws and Regulations'—deals with the legal and regulatory issues of different sectors of hard infrastructure such as power, telecom, rail, air, road and sea in India. These are the sector-specific legal and regulatory mandatory requirements and have evolved mainly in the last two decades or so.

Private participation in infrastructure building in the country is in its nascent stage; hence, most of the developments have been on the basis of the experiences of the developed world which have been adapted to the Indian conditions and, thereafter, being amended and modified as the country is moving on the learning curve. The third chapter—'Laws and Regulations across Sectors'—discusses some of the regulatory mechanisms and legal provisions which are applicable to all the infrastructure projects irrespective of the sectors. The chapter discusses the interplay between law and economics, and how regulation is important in cases of market failure, and elaborates that a proper legal framework with effective regulations is necessary to monitor and regulate the creation and management of public goods.

The fourth chapter—'Challenges to Infrastructure Development in India'—talks about numerous challenges being faced by infrastructure projects and PPPs in India. Mainly, these are related to land acquisition and environmental clearance besides several other requirements which are applicable to almost any contract or project in the country. The fifth chapter—'Funding and Legal Framework'—deals with issues related to funding the infrastructure projects and how PPPs have suffered because of lack of confidence of investors in funding long-term projects. Change in the legal environment with stricter and tighter borrowing and lending laws—mainly the Insolvency and Bankruptcy Code (IBC), 2016—has resulted in a sense of urgency and sharper sense of purpose while lending and borrowing money for PPP infrastructure projects, which are usually for a long duration of time.

The sixth chapter—'Judiciary and Infrastructure'—discusses the role of judiciary at all levels from the district court to the high court to the Supreme Court, in PPPs and infrastructure contracts. The role of the courts and judges is critical in not getting any of the infrastructure projects delayed beyond a reasonable time limit as stay orders can be highly damaging when public interest litigations (PILs) are filed to oppose—on one pretext or the other—so many infrastructure projects.

Easy accessibility to courts is, at times, being misused by business competitors and publicity-hungry individuals. The seventh chapter—'Political Will and Intention'—strongly highlights the importance of political patronage, along with bureaucratic backing, for the PPPs and infrastructure projects to reach a logical conclusion. Without political support, it is almost impossible to have a successful completion of any infrastructure project. Democracy brings in its own peculiar advantages and challenges, and a business executive in the infrastructure sector must be able to appreciate them fully to be effective.

In almost all the chapters, I have written about certain practical aspects—both from managerial and legal perspectives—that a business executive, as well as a practising lawyer, will find useful while dealing with such issues. Each chapter ends with a few key takeaways, which, I'm sure, will prove to be quite helpful for executives. I learnt and picked up most of these things during my law practice days in Babuji's chambers while having long discussions with my *gurubhais* (fellow students in a *gurukul*). Notable among them are Shri Alok Sinha—Babuji's son, Shri Virendra Mishra, Shri Upendra Mishra, Justice Saurabh Lavania, Shri Subhash Vidyarthi, Shri Manish Singh and Shri Agendra Sinha—Babuji's grandson. Thanks to each one of them for enlightening deliberations, usually over a cup of tea, and under Babuji's watchful eyes.

I would like to thank Ms Mathews and Ms Kathait from SAGE for their constant support and valuable comments. Thanks to my family—Manjari, Anant and Akshat—for encouraging me to work on the manuscript of the book even during difficult times and odd hours.

Anurag K. Agarwal
Indian Institute of Management
Ahmedabad

Chapter 1

INTRODUCTION

It was beyond imagination to think a restaurant at the Bombay International Airport could give rise to one of the most important Supreme Court judgements. During the national emergency from 1975 to 1977, the International Airport Authority at Bombay, now known as Mumbai, decided to have a good restaurant in its premises to serve the passengers and for this very purpose it invited tenders from competent parties. It massively became the most talked case study related to the expansion of the role of administrative law in India as well as a sort of a highly recommended treatise on the role of the State in infrastructure development.

It so happened that hoteliers of tier 1 were permitted to submit their bids and hoteliers of tier 2, 3 and others were ineligible for participating in the bidding process. As luck would have it, there was no hotelier who could clear the stipulated requirements. However, a bidder from a certain lower tier, who had taken the chance of submitting the bid despite not being eligible in the first instance, got the contract.

Other interested parties from the lower tier, who were also interested but had not participated because of the conditions laid down earlier, felt aggrieved and filed a petition in the court that on the basis of equality—as protected under the fundamental rights in the Constitution of India—they should have also been given a chance to participate in the bidding process. And as that chance was not given to them, the contract which had already been awarded must be terminated and fresh bidding should be initiated.

This was the period just after the Emergency, and the courts in India, particularly the Supreme Court, were trying to bring back the balance of power. For the judiciary, it became an issue of high importance and a trial of Indian judiciary prowess. In 1973, the Supreme Court had made the landmark decision that the 'basic structure' of the Constitution of India could not be changed by the legislature. This was the historic judgement in Kesavananda Bharati case,[1] decided by a 13-judge bench, which to a large extent strengthened the foundation of judicial review in India.

The power of judicial review, according to the Constitution of India, is one of the most important restraint on the legislature and the executive, and thus, the interpretation of the Constitution for this purpose was done by the Supreme Court in a new way—though not fully inconsistent with earlier pronouncements—which was the dawn of a new era of judicial activism. It may not exactly be judicial activism, but one can definitely call it the beginning of a period of 'judicial assertion'. It was made clear by this and other judgements of that time that the government, whether at the centre or in the states, must work within the constitutional framework, whose limits would be determined according to the interpretation of the periphery of the constitutional boundaries, which sometimes appear to be fuzzy, but with the free, fair and fearless judiciary the boundaries got perceptible clarity.

This was the case of *Ramana Dayaram Shetty v. The International Airport Authority*,[2] and we will discuss this case in great detail later in the book. It gave a new dimension to the discussion about the constitutional issues and infrastructure.

---

[1] *Kesavananda Bharati Sripadagalvaru and Ors. v. State of Kerala and Anr.*, (1973) 4 SCC 225.
[2] Supreme Court of India, 4 May 1979, Bench: Bhagwati, P.N., Tulzapurkar, V.D., and Pathak, R.S., JJ.; 1979 AIR 1628, 1979 SCR (3)1014.

CONSTITUTIONAL MANDATE AND INFRASTRUCTURE

Remarkably, the Constitution of India in Part IV—the Directive Principles of State Policy—talks about those provisions which are not enforceable in any court of law but are necessary to be the fundamental principles in the governance of the country, and making it the duty of the State to follow them as the guiding light while formulating policies and executing them. In brief, these directive principles aim at creating a secure social order with equality and providing all sort of support to the people of India so that they can reach their full potential and collectively work towards the growth and development of the country.

For this purpose, adequate infrastructure—both physical and social—is the prerequisite and it is the bounden duty of the State to create that infrastructure. Significantly, the resources at the disposal of the State are always inadequate—and that is not the position only in India but is true for most of the countries in the world except maybe a very few countries—for example, Brunei, Qatar, Switzerland, Finland, Canada, etc., where the resources are in surplus and it is a question of prioritizing the use of available resources.

Despite the rapid urbanization in the last six decades or so, more than two-thirds of Indians live in rural areas depending heavily on agriculture. While thinking about the condition of people living in the rural areas, one may immediately either romanticize the lush green fields with the hero and heroine merrily running around singing a melodious song, à la Bollywood, or think about the poverty, illiteracy, helplessness and vulnerability of the hapless rural folk as they did in the black and white movies of yesteryears.

Somehow, a balanced view of how the villages of India really look like after seven decades of independence is missed by most of the people at the top of this thinking pyramid—readers, writers, policymakers, bureaucrats, bankers, intellectuals, social workers, reformers, activists, engineers, doctors, lawyers and so many others. Moreover, it is highly important that they have a clear idea as to how the Indian villages should look like.

It is not at all necessary that villages in India should look the same as they are in Switzerland or the countryside in England. To use the overstated statement that the 'soul of India lives in villages'—but nothing else may capture it so well, and that's why I have no qualms in using this statement—it is not fair to compare the villages in India with the villages of any other country, especially in any developed country. It would not be accurate or justified to say that the villages in India are the concentration of poverty, illiteracy, unemployment and everything deplorable one can think of. On the contrary, the prime economy of the country is based on the regular routine life in villages which really makes the life of the billion plus people in India worth living. The life in the villages is still closer to Mother Nature and people get to breathe in unpolluted air, see greenery all around and enjoy huge open spaces.

It may sound a bit too romantic, however, as compared to urban living, the villages surely provide a more holistic and physically active life. The daily routine itself is full of exercise, right from the dawn to late in the night. But, there are serious problems also. Most of them are dependent on agriculture and related activities. Though there is a lot of scope for expansion and development of agriculture with new techniques of farming, there is often the problem of increase in family size resulting in smaller land holdings with successive generations. Nonetheless, a large rural population keeps working to make the best of the available resources and get maximum returns with hope for a better tomorrow. The biggest hurdle is inadequate infrastructure.

Proper and effective connectivity between the villages and the urban centres, and among the villages themselves, is extremely important for the two-way process regarding policy formulation and implementation, and getting realistic inputs from the villages to the urban centres. The desired impact can be made possible only if there is physical connectivity through roads, rail network, river and canal network, and maybe a little too ambitious but even with air connectivity by using small choppers, especially as medical ambulance and in times of disasters and distress.

The physical connectivity is something very basic and it has been discussed, debated, protested against, vehemently argued for, used and abused, exploited as a source for siphoning of public funds, witnessed poor quality of public works and has seen unscrupulous contractors and public servants flourishing while the public suffered. The Nandi Infrastructure Corridor Enterprise (NICE), also known as the Bengaluru–Mysuru Infrastructure Corridor (BMIC), is a case in point. It became a major issue of corruption, delay and inefficiency since the planning of the project started. Jalandhar–Amritsar Highway has attracted controversies regarding misuse of land acquisition laws, underpayment and protest by farmers. This is the situation in many parts of the country where rural and urban connectivity is planned and executed.

Thanks to the fast developments in technology, telecommunications through mobile networks has reached almost every village in the country without bothering about laying telephone lines physically. However, that is not true about power, and the ideal situation of 24×7 power availability to every village in the country is still a distant dream. Bringing a railhead somewhere near every village may not be required now as the emphasis is on making roads connecting the villagers with a tertiary road connectivity network linking with the arterial road system and thereby reducing to a large extent or almost eliminating dependency on railways. The network of rivers and canals is typically either absent in the country or, even if present in some parts of the country, it is in a pathetic state due to silting and heavy pollution. Something similar is also happening in Indian urban space, however, with much more speed and gusto.

URBANIZATION AND SMART CITIES

Urbanization is a global phenomenon and India is also witnessing it in a major way. Almost one-third of the Indian population lives in cities and urban areas are growing rapidly. With this state of affairs, the situation in urban areas regarding infrastructure and facilities available to the people living in the city is pathetic. Even in the old cities which have been the centres of civilization not for decades but for centuries, the facilities are either deteriorating or not keeping pace with rapid changes in technology and standards of living in most of the developed world. At times, it is dismal to see people in major urban centres in India struggling to live in a peaceful and balanced manner where they can sustain themselves and simultaneously enjoy life. It can simply be said that life is a constant struggle for them living in these cities. Urban infrastructure is not just a matter for the government to be maintained and created but also the responsibility of the people who live there to develop, nurture and let it grow according to the changing aspirations and needs of the future generations.

And that is where precisely the role of PPP is along with the rural areas. It is to be seen that cities need to be capable enough of giving its people workable environment and also have a good balance between their working and non-working activities. It is not possible for any country, even with all the resources at its disposal, to transform existing infrastructure in most of the urban areas instantaneously by using a magic wand as it requires time. Rome was definitely not built in a day! It becomes even more difficult, or almost impossible, for countries with meagre resources as more time and efforts are spent in garnering resources and getting consent of the concerned people in a democratic set-up. Thus, it is important to prioritize certain areas in a particular city or certain cities in the entire country—and not all the cities together—to be transformed in the first phase.

For this very purpose, the Government of India (GoI) started the Smart Cities project which aims at using smart techniques which mean modern mechanisms of technology, management and governance to create sustainable cities with minimum usage of resources like energy and provide the greatest benefit to the people. Now it is to be seen whether with the word 'smart' this entire project is only a rhetoric or actually worthy of being called truly smart. It may require strong political will to take the project forward without being affected by change in any government, whether at the centre or at the state level, and also not worrying too much about the resources needed to complete the project in time and as envisaged.

A good number of cities have been chosen in the country for this very purpose and a large number of people, especially city planners, administrators, technical experts, architects and others are all brought together to work in a concerted manner to provide the best for the particular zonal areas of these cities so that they can be created as either model zones or model cities which can be replicated in the rest of the country. There can be many administrative and legal issues involved. However, the current legal environment in the country may provide some level of confidence to the persons involved in the implementation of the concerned laws which shall be done with the purpose of achieving the pre-decided goal, rather than creating hurdles in the path of infrastructure development in the urban areas.

The mission of creating 100 smart cities across the country is to be done as a concerted effort between the central government and the state governments. The fundamental idea is to develop certain islands of sustainable development and citizen-friendly administration in an ocean of filth and squalor so that slowly but surely the developmental effect of these islands positively impacts the adjoining towns and cities. For this purpose, it has been taken into consideration that the smart cities chosen in the first cohort—20 in number—are geographically spread throughout the country and are already fairly developed and have the capability and potential to be developed further, both in expansion and the quality of life for the existing place.

It is roughly a five-year plan and it would be a pleasant surprise for everyone if it can be accomplished within that period of time. In most of such projects, time and cost overrun are the two most important problems and as this mission is the brainchild of the government of the day, it may not get the same backing if there is another party or coalition in power after a certain period of time. Thus, continuance of policy formulation and implementation for a longish period of time is vital for the success of this mission.

BRIDGING THE SOCIAL AND ECONOMIC GAP

The infrastructure plays an important role in bridging the social and economic gap in the country which has been extremely wide for several decades and centuries. Since independence, a number of efforts have been made; however, the lack of proper social and physical infrastructure has been a major constraint in retaining and, at times, widening it. Since the liberalization of the economy in 1991 and thereafter, there has been immense private participation in the creation of infrastructure and being participative in a number of business activities, which hitherto were meant only for the government.

Aviation has been one of them and in the last two decades and a little more this sector has seen tremendous change, the most appreciable being the ease with which the middle class of the country is considering air travel as normal, affordable and well within their perception. Now, air travel is not considered to be a luxury; it still hasn't been brought in the category of being one of the necessities of life; however, it is definitely a convenience which many people in the country are frequently enjoying.

This has been possible primarily due to the change in the policy, which is related to aviation in the country, and also due to the private participation in running airlines on commercial basis and pumping in money for creation of world-class airports. This has been no minor achievement in the period of a quarter of a century. Higher passenger movement and aircraft movement are considered to be two of the important parameters for considering data for determining the development of an economy, and by this yardstick, India is doing pretty well with passengers demanding better infrastructure and modern facilities. Private investment has undoubtedly been the driving force in the phenomenal growth of aviation in India. Despite issues related to land acquisition and numerous court cases, aviation has been a game changer in infrastructure with major construction company vying with each other to get a slice of the cake in the form of contracts and licenses.

Institutional and other investors have always been quite large hearted in supporting aviation leading to the Indian Railways and road transport companies. They are compelled to fight for survival as far as the top segment of travellers is concerned. Emergence of the tier 2 cities on the aviation map can surely be said to be resurgence of a major segment of the Indian population. It was previously on the periphery of developments made in the transport sector. Several of the private airlines, usually called as the no-frills airlines with a little bit touch of condescend and ridicule, are directly connecting so many of the second tier of cities, without following the hub and spoke model. Thus, they provide greater freedom and several options to the passengers to choose from while making a decision for travel.

Development of infrastructure related to health and education is essential for the long-term benefits to percolate to the bottom of the pyramid in society. Blending of public and private participation has been successfully experienced for the last several decades in many parts of the country. There may not be unanimity about the success of the effectiveness of private participation in certain areas, and public participation in some other areas, however, it can easily be observed that in most of the big cities there has been almost equal participation of public and private, with the private maybe gaining dominance of in the last two decades or so. Somehow, private participation has not been that much in tier 2 towns, smaller cities and villages. The reason is quite obvious: ROI and the potential to make profit. Therefore, people in these places have been looking towards the State for provision of health, education, sanitation, etc.

Lack of private investment has made the situation worse for people living in these areas as the State has not been able to provide the basic necessary infrastructure leading to discontentment among the people and absence of education and health care of the least possible standards. This absence has resulted in a vicious cycle of letting people remain illiterate and unhealthy, negatively impacting their chances of being employed and able to earn a living, and thereby diminishing their chances of being educated and leading a healthy life. Long-term social goals can only be achieved when basic education and primary health care are available to each and every person, whether living in a village or town, or city. For this to make possible, creation of physical infrastructure is a prerequisite.

E-GOVERNANCE: TRANSPARENCY AND ACCOUNTABILITY

In a democratic system, it is of utmost importance that public works are done in a transparent manner and the contractors are made accountable to the people, though not directly but indirectly, through a committee of responsible persons or body of persons oriented towards public welfare and social good. It's always not desirable to contest any such matter in a court of law, even if the judicial process is speedy and inexpensive, as intervention of legal machinery has the possibility of bringing in vogue any other plausible interpretation to the black letter policy or law, which might be technically possible but not truly in the spirit of a welfare state. To avoid most of these obstructions later on in the life of a project, it is advisable that the process of granting the licence or a contract or any other approval or permission by the State must be completely transparent with the players being treated equally.

The efforts by the government in creating e-governance portals have been laudable, and information sharing along with submission of tenders has become less cumbersome, boosting the confidence of investors, contractors and other business persons in general. 'Knowledge is power', an old quote by Francis Bacon has today relevantly transformed itself into 'information is power'. Previously, only the people close to the government of the day were able to get the right information at the right time and would typically use it for their sole interest, and at times they were also able to create barriers so that that information may not be known to its competitors. Now with a lot many things available on the internet, the government is making efforts that complete information regarding new construction projects, the specifications, requirements from different contractors, notice inviting tender, request for proposal (RfP), etc., are done in an electronic manner, with an intent of avoiding the middlemen and different modes of communication channels, which ordinarily did not work always to the satisfaction of the parties.

The e-governance initiative has been, one can say with a certain high level of confidence, quite successful in bringing out the nation from the dark ages where hardly any information was available to all the interested parties to an era where the floodgates have opened and too much information is available at the click of a mouse to almost everyone. Now, it depends on the initiative taken by the private parties in accessing, analysing and commercially exploiting whatever information is available. Along with the e-governance initiative, the Right to Information Act, 2005, has been a very potent tool in the hands of business persons who desire of doing business with the government. Independent and fearless judiciary in the country has always come to the rescue of the hapless contractors against the might of the State. However, there have been several instances of unscrupulous private parties taking the not-so-helpless State to different legal fora resulting in inordinate delay of the completion of projects and sometimes bringing the infrastructure projects to a screeching halt for an indefinite period of time.

To harness the resources for completion of projects so the public can be benefited, technology can play a major role. However, it is essential that the cutting-edge technology should be used along with making the stakeholders aware about it, so as to enable them to be a part of the transparent procedure. The digital divide, which is usually created between the empowered and un-empowered due to either lack of resources, of accessibility, or lack of both, can be damaging in making opportunities available in an equitable manner. The government said centre and the states have recognized the importance of making everyone digitally literate and also providing accessibility to the digital content using a smartphone and fast internet connection. For this purpose as well, it was realized quite realistically that it cannot be done by the State alone, or for that matter the State by itself was in no position to do so.

Private initiative, in bridging the digital gap and thus bringing technology at the doorstep, in fact in the hands of each and every citizen of the country, has been very well recognized and financially rewarded by the people themselves, in the form of increasing internet and call plan subscriptions. Several of the private companies have taken the risk of heavily subsidizing both handsets and connectivity charges enabling the people to use them and, consecutively, expanding the user base, so that the business model results in profits after a certain reasonable period of time.

PPP: LAW AND ECONOMICS

PPPs work through contracts, and contracts need to be mutually beneficial for both the parties—and all the parties in a contract with more than two parties—to be sustainable and successful in the long run. Most of the PPPs are for a longish period of time with the concession agreement (CA) signed for 20 years or more in the case of highways, airports, seaports, etc. It is essential that the parties maintain interest in the contracts over that period of time, and that is possible only when there is a continual flow of—even if in small amount—benefit to them, either in monetary terms or otherwise, in the form of creation of public value, enhancement in brand value and goodwill.

The close relationship of law and economics, also discussed as economic analysis of law, can best be seen in action through PPP contracts. The transaction costs and incentive mechanism play a major role in the success or failure of effective contract enforcement. Contractual norms, tightened using the basic understanding of economics and law, often go a long way in value creation without excessive risk of matters being disputed in a court of law. Many a time, as experienced in India, tender process is marred from the very beginning by litigation, resulting in stalling the project. Despite the best intentions of the parties (the State and the private contractor), the matters are not able to be taken forward, as circuitous legal proceedings leave hardly any scope for settlements because the actors on behalf of the State are in no position to proactively settle the issue or even forget about it and move on.

Law, according to the British philosopher John Austin and the positive school, is the command of sovereign along with the threat of punishment. The economic rational man works towards his well-being. The element of morality takes a back seat; however, law, somehow, has an inbuilt element of morality, howsoever minuscule it may be. This tension between application of legal principles with morality embedded in it, and interpreting and adjudicating on the basis of economic analysis, brings forth extremely interesting situations which differ from jurisdiction to jurisdiction. Also, the treatment given to the subject depends on individual perception and often—though undesirable—biases which are typically explained and justified as experience, discretion, multi-view of at times the so-called simple and objective problems, or the open-and-shut cases.

The basic purpose of entering into a contract is to get the ability to seek a legal remedy in case promise is broken; however, it is important to understand that under what conditions this can be satisfied, that is, when a contract can be enforced. It appears to be simple but in infrastructure projects it becomes extremely difficult to prove as both the parties try their best to wriggle out of the situation. Mutually beneficial transactions, as discussed earlier, result in better enforcement. The most important principle in contract law, from the economic perspective, is the aspect of consideration which is essential to be present to make a contract valid, though the courts do not go into the adequacy or inadequacy of consideration for a particular transaction. This is based on the fundamental voluntary nature, absolutely free consent, of the parties to the contract.

In long-term infrastructure contracts, there is a possibility of asymmetry of information as certain insiders working in the government, or in close relationship with the government, get to know a lot many things which others may not have access to and, therefore, it is imperative that the parties are treated equally with all efforts made to eliminate the possibility of asymmetric information. It is also to be considered that the infrastructure creation is socially valuable and economically viable for the State. It cannot be accepted that contracts do not create long-term social value but result in crony capitalism leading to feathering of the nest of some favourite persons.

Thus, the situation becomes far more difficult in egalitarian societies where the State is bound to provide a level playing field with access to information to anyone interested in infrastructure projects. Often there are issues of 'means and ends'[3] of government projects regarding the concerns for land acquisition and the specific use of the inputs. Public use and public good are usually interpreted in different ways to justify the mobilization of resources, formulation of policies and execution of plans made. Judicial intervention is justified on the grounds of ensuring absence of any coercive means by the State in implementation.

REGULATORY ISSUES IN INFRASTRUCTURE

Infrastructure development heavily depends on proper regulatory bodies functioning in professional manner so that private players get a level playing field, and the regulatory mechanism ensures balance between the control of the State and social good along with reasonable returns for the private player. It is a tightrope walk for the regulatory bodies as

---

[3] Thomas Merrill, 'The Economics of Public Use', *Cornell Law Review* 72 (1986): 61–116.

tilting heavily in favour of the people may result in lower tariffs but making the business conditions extremely unfavourable for the private player, which obviously will result in erosion of interest in the business, and thereby decline in the service provided. On the other hand, if the regulator is similarly inclined in favour of the private player, it will result in shoddy services for the people and filling in the coffers of the private players unjustifiably.

Regulators in most of the evolved jurisdictions brought top professionals from the concerned subject matter, experts from law, economics, policy formulation, administration, finance, management, etc. Typically, regulatory bodies are created according to the provisions of the governing law—mostly by statute enacted by the competent legislative body, whether the central legislature or the state legislature in federal countries like India—and have to work within the framework of the governing statute. Interestingly, this statute needs to be interpreted within the constitutional framework and whenever there is a conflict or confusion regarding the periphery of the statute, it has to be interpreted by the judiciary keeping in mind the basic principles applicable in the concerned jurisdiction. In India, the ultimate test is the test of public interest or public welfare.

Regulating bodies, usually, have the powers of the lawmaking—generally making of regulations and rules—and execution in day-to-day matters. Remarkably, certain adjudicatory powers are also vested on the regulators along with the creation of an appellate authority to decide on appeals made by the aggrieved parties. It is a matter of serious concern that in India in the last two or three decades, a large number of regulatory bodies have been created; however, there is a dearth of qualified and competent professionals to man the positions in these bodies as there is normally a great attraction for the same individuals to be poached by the private players at the remuneration which is much higher as compared to what is offered at the regulatory institutions.

As India has been a little late in the creation of regulatory institutions, it can learn several things from the evolved jurisdictions, particularly in the developed countries, which have their own regulatory mechanisms and those have been working with fair amount of sources. The USA and the UK are two major beacons, of course, with several stories of inefficient functioning and failure also, of good regulatory mechanisms which can be the guiding lights for Indian regulatory bodies. There are, however, two major issues which need to be kept in mind while making any comparison between regulatory institutions in India and those in the USA and the UK—monetary resources and population. Undoubtedly, the resources at the disposal of the developed world are much higher as compared to that of India and the population to which they cater is much smaller as compared to that of in India. Though the basic principles remain the same anywhere in the world, there has to be a different treatment given to several policy and implementation issues in India.

On most of the occasions, the government and the judiciary in India are cognizant of this fact and have not blindly copied the Western model, yet at times there is an urge to align the Indian regulatory institutions on the lines of the Western counterparts. A few important reasons are the well-established nature of the Western institutions and a very high level of advocacy and concerted efforts to connect with the peers and like-minded persons all over the world. Investment of time and effort in research-related activities and publications has also been major factors for the wide acceptability of the style of working of most of the regulatory bodies in the developed world. Indian conditions are different and, therefore, the same method of working may not be truly effective in reaching a balance between the private players' interests and public welfare.

There is a continuous need for bringing in regulatory reforms to make the regulatory institutions updated and relevant in the fast-changing business environment, especially the use of the latest technology and financial methods. Measuring public good and public welfare is also not easy as it is not simply a numerical exercise but has to be worked using numerous factors, which make the infrastructure project socially relevant and effectively enforceable.

In the chapters that follow, we will discuss how the legal and regulatory environment for infrastructure development has facilitated or obstructed the speedy enforcement of the plans for creation of the requisite infrastructure. With the help of case studies of decided court judgements and several other very well-known stories in the business and legal fraternity, we will try to understand various infrastructure sectors such as roads, highways, railways, ports, airports, power and telecom. Role of the government and the courts shall be analysed with decided cases and also several cases which although have not been finally decided in the courts of law, yet have been the talk of the town for mostly wrong reasons.

Financial institutions and other lenders have been reluctant to put in money in several infrastructure projects due to high level of uncertainty—political, economic and legal. Whether emerging challenges are surmountable or not is a question at the top of mind of almost everyone dealing with infrastructure directly or with issues related to infrastructure. The better the readers such as the executives dealing with infrastructure remain informed, the more the chances of their success in tackling evolving issues.

KEY TAKEAWAYS

- *Urbanization:* India has witnessed very rapid urbanization in the last few decades and the trend is expected to continue in the future giving rise to excessive demand of good infrastructure. Thus, the demand shall be very high which cannot be taken care of by the government. Role of private sector shall be important in the task of nation building.

- *Rule of law:* The legal and administrative arrangements for providing adequate infrastructure shall be governed by the law of the land, and hence rule of law in allocation and enforcement of contracts shall remain vital to ensure fairness and judicious exercise of discretionary power. Courts have a very special role in upholding rule of law.

- *Aspirational levels:* The levels of aspiration of Indians, both in urban and rural areas, are quite high and usually growth in different sectors of infrastructure falls short of the aspirations of the people of India, and hence it is desirable to bridge the gap by providing better infrastructure. The entire efforts of the democratically elected governments are to do well in the eyes of the people of India. Business executives, while working towards profit-making, must keep the rising levels of ambitions of the people in India.

Chapter 2
SECTORAL LAWS AND REGULATIONS

Infrastructure may have different meanings, the most common understanding being that of something necessary, which can be called as hard infrastructure, and others being supportive in nature and can be termed as soft infrastructure. In the former category, one can consider buildings, roads, highways, bridges, tunnels, rivers, power, airports, seaports, telecommunication, water supply, drainage, etc. These are the things which are primary in nature and without their existence it is difficult, if not impossible, to think of human survival in a civilized fashion. What and how much of different sectors of infrastructure are needed depend on what time of human civilization we are considering. For instance, several thousands of years ago during the earliest human civilizations, namely Chinese, Nile River in Egypt, Indus Valley, Mesopotamian, etc., the needs were rudimentary, still dwelling units were needed with proper mechanism for ingress and egress, well-defined streets, drainage system and seaports or river banks, depending on the particular geographical location.

In today's scenario, besides the things mentioned, power, telecommunication and internet connectivity have to be added for civilized living even in rural areas. The needs, of course, vary from rural to semi-urban to urban to big metros. Agrarian economies also depend a lot on proper infrastructure. It is interesting to note that the word infrastructure itself is made of two words: infra and structure; the former meaning below, and the latter loosely meaning something which has been built using different parts. It was in France in the latter part of the 19th century that the word infrastructure was used for something which was below or under the buildings, railways, etc. It could have been the underground sewer, drainage pipes, gas pipes, water pipes, etc. However, over the years, the word 'infrastructure' has been expanded to include things which are not only under the ground but also above the ground.

Besides the primary infrastructure as mentioned earlier, the supporting infrastructure in most jurisdictions includes the organizations and institutions meant to take care of different aspects of society including health, education, economy, law and order, culture, disaster management, emergency services, legal environment, leisure and entertainment, travel, tourism, etc. The ambit of the word infrastructure, thus, is very wide and is purported to include each and everything which makes life worth living. Betterment of infrastructure can be done either by the government or by private initiative. There can be even the model of combining the government and private, and, therefore, making it a partnership between the government and private, popularly known as PPP. Infrastructure can be said to be something fundamental for human beings.

In this chapter, we will be confining ourselves to certain sectors of infrastructure which are critical in nature for the development of the country and well-being of the people. These are the major sectors and include power, telecommunication, railways, air travel, roads and sea. There are surely several other very important sectors such as rivers, water supply, drainage, sewerage, waste management, focusing exclusively on urban transport, dams and canals for irrigation, but we will be discussing legal and regulatory issues sector-wise for the sectors mentioned hereinbefore.

ROADS

Since 1947, when India became independent, the needs of the people of the country have changed and are continuously changing. This change is guided by the growing aspirations of the people, which truly is a reflection of the welfare state in which we all live, rather than the police state under the British rule which was more concerned with collection of revenue, maintaining law and order internally and protecting the international boundaries from external aggression. At the time of Independence, the country was at a crossroads: either to follow the rural economy strictly or align itself with the Western model of development. The country prudently chose a mixed model giving due recognition to the thousands of years of Indian tradition and culture, which had been nurtured with great care in the real rural India, and aspiring to achieve the glorious heights of development already reached in the first-world countries, that is, the developed world.

The question as to who would do it, whether the government or the private sector alone, was also answered by following the middle path of getting the best of both the worlds in the shape of mixed economy, with both public sector and private sector playing complementary roles in moving ahead harmoniously on the path of development. Connecting people in far-flung areas in a continental size country like India through a network of roads has always been one of the most important and obvious objectives of governments, both at the centre and in the states; however, it has been an excruciatingly slow process.

CASE STUDY

NHAI v. Gwalior Jhansi Expressway Ltd, SC, 2018[4]

Between the neighbouring states of Uttar Pradesh and Madhya Pradesh, there was a need to widen the two-lane portion of about 80 km length to four-lane portion as the traffic between certain major cities in the two states had been on the rise and it had been anticipated that the existing road would not have been able to cater to the ever-increasing traffic. With this purpose, the National Highways Authority of India (NHAI), which had been created under the NHAI Act, 1988, and entrusted with the responsibility of making and maintaining highways in the country, entered into a CA with Gwalior Jhansi Expressway Ltd (the concessionaire) in 2006. That was the time when the United Progressive Alliance (UPA) 1 was in power at the centre with Dr Manmohan Singh as the prime minister for the first term, from 2004 to 2009.

The CA provided all the details regarding specifications, different milestones for completion of work and also details about the payments to be made. Less than two-thirds of the work was done till 2012 when the NHAI issued a Cure Period Notice (a notice to the party anticipated to be close to breach of contract, but breach has not occurred; thus, it is a warning to the other party to perform urgently or face legal action for breach of the contract) to the concessionaire. The concessionaire refuted the notice and denied the allegations made. It also moved the court seeking a stay order on the said notice and any future termination order. The Delhi High Court passed an interim stay in 2014, and later in 2015, the matter was referred to arbitration for resolution of this business dispute.

---

[4] *National Highways Authority of India v. Gwalior Jhansi Expressway Limited,* Supreme Court of India, 13 July 2018, Bench: A. M. Khanwilkar, Dipak Misra, Dr D. Y. Chandrachud, JJ., 2018 Indlaw SC 492; Civil Appeal No. 3288 of 2018.

So the fact of the matter was that the construction of the road had stopped and the people were not getting the benefit of the widening of the road as envisaged. Legal proceedings were on and the NHAI and the concessionaire both separately requested the arbitral tribunal to allow each of them to complete the work. The NHAI was interested in getting the work completed, preferably by another contractor; however, the concessionaire was interested to complete the remaining part of the work by taking partial risk but in the long run keeping its record clean of completing a project it had taken up. Somehow, the end result of getting the project completed was common for both parties but the methods of getting it done were not aligned.

An interesting thing to note is that by this time, that is, 2015 and thereafter, the UPA government was out of power in the centre, as the National Democratic Alliance (NDA) came to power in the centre in 2014. Non-completion of an important project was creating avoidable issues for the political leaders, and efforts were made both at political and bureaucratic levels to somehow get the matter settled and move on towards project completion. With this thought in mind, multi-party negotiations were held with the government, the NHAI, concessionaire and other stakeholders. However, legal issues of the proceedings at the arbitral tribunal had to be taken care of before any progress could be made in the real sense.

During the arbitration proceedings, the NHAI conditionally offered to provide funds for the completion of the project in a time-bound manner. The concessionaire did not agree to all the conditions of the offer made by the NHAI, which led to a request made by the NHAI to withdraw its offer. The arbitral tribunal did not allow the withdrawal of the offer made by the NHAI. Taking note of the interests of the public, lenders and the concessionaire, the arbitral tribunal observed an interim order of 2016 that as the concessionaire had unconditionally accepted the offer made by the NHAI, the work should proceed further towards completion of the project, and it did not make sense to award the remaining contract work to a construction company, other than the concessionaire who already had clear understanding and experience of the work required to be done.

In a tripartite meeting between the government, the NHAI and the concessionaire, it had been tried to find the right balance so as to arrive at a win-win solution with minimum financial burden and risk on either of the parties. The arbitral tribunal ordered that the concessionaire would have the right of first refusal (RoFR) to match the lowest bid in case of fresh bidding for the remaining work. Whether the concessionaire was supposed to take part in any such bidding process or not was not mentioned in the arbitral tribunal's order. It was completely silent on this aspect.

The NHAI issued a tender for the remaining work in November 2016 inviting technical and financial bids and clearly mentioned that the concessionaire shall have the ROFR, that is, the rights to match the lowest bid, if it was a responsive bidder. Details were provided regarding technical specifications and the procedure to be followed for the award of the contract. The concessionaire did not take part in the bidding process, and when the NHAI was in the final stage of awarding the contract in April 2017, it sought permission from the arbitral tribunal to complete the balance work under the belief that it would have got the chance of matching the lowest bid.

The NHAI contested it on the primary ground that the concessionaire chose to remain silent and did not participate in the bidding process, and, hence, it did not have any right to be given the chance to match the lowest bid as it had waived its RoFR. The arbitral tribunal, in its wisdom, decided the matter in favour of the concessionaire, mainly following the rationale that the concessionaire had done the lion's share of work and hence it should be given the chance to complete the remaining portion of the work, and also that by not giving the remaining work to the concessionaire, there would be creation of avoidable confusion and chaos. According to the arbitral tribunal, the fact that the concessionaire did not take part in the bidding process was immaterial.

The NHAI filed an appeal against this decision in the Delhi High Court, which upheld the arbitral tribunal's decision. Aggrieved by that decision, the NHAI appealed in the Supreme Court. From the public interest perspective, the matter has been pending for years and precious public resources have been blocked without any benefit to the public. This matter has been going to different judicial forums—arbitral tribunal, high court, the Supreme Court, etc.—and has also undergone through the administrative scrutiny of various government committees. Despite so many steps undertaken, the road has still not been constructed and the parties had been going through a fierce legal battle apparently to take control of the one-third portion of the four-lane highway.

The Supreme Court's decision was principally based on legal principles of awarding a contract to the bidding process along with the mandate of an arbitral tribunal as decided by the parties to a contract. It is a very well-settled principle of law that the arbitrators are a creation of the contract and are bound to work within the periphery of authority given to them by the parties. In any case, they cannot go beyond that very periphery and it goes without saying that while making any decision they cannot violate any principle of law. The fundamental principle of contract law regarding the bidding process is that the terms and conditions as mentioned in the invitation for bids have to be followed strictly, with only one caveat that they have to be in consonance with the law of the land and public policy as prevalent at any given time. By no stretch of imagination, any of the parties can have the freedom to transgress the set terms and conditions.

In a detailed judgement in July 2018, the Supreme Court decided on the basis of the fundamental principles of law and distinguishing some of the previous judgement cited by both the parties in support of their respective arguments that the arbitral tribunals went beyond its powers in deciding that the concessionaire should be given the RoFR even if it hadn't taken part in the bidding process, which was made mandatory according to the terms and conditions of the bidding document inviting bids. The concessionaire could have very easily taken part in the bidding process, and thereafter it would have been possible to give it the option of matching the lowest bid, however, as it chose, for reasons best known to it, not to participate in the process it would not be proper, according to the law, to give it a chance to match the lowest bid.

If the decision is made in favour of the concessionaire, it would be like allowing it to have its cake and eat it too. The Supreme Court came heavily on the arbitral tribunal and also the Delhi High Court for ignoring the obvious facts of the case and the situation in which decision had to be made. It was a grave error on their part to ignore the basic terms and conditions of the bidding process as mentioned by the NHAI in its invitation for bids, which were termed to be quite reasonable and practical under the given circumstances of getting the work completed speedily and effectively in public interest.

The purpose with which the NHAI had been created seems to be lost as there are inordinate delays in getting the work done by private parties in the form of a PPP. The legal rigmarole and political decision-making have on several occasions made the fundamental reason for the formation of any contract—a CA in case of a PPP—simply being overlooked. The parties to the contract have been insisting on their legal rights as the gains from the contract may not appear to be coming to them within a reasonable period of time and the parties— interestingly both the parties at the same time—believe that they have been wronged, and the only legal recourse will be able to set the things correct.

Due to the strong insistence on the intricate legal language and going into the finer aspects of the language used in the contract, which might not have been the intention of the parties in detail while they had been making up their minds to enter into the contract at the time of a dispute, usually makes the going very tough and any negotiation, or rather re-negotiation at that stage, becomes next to impossible. In the instant case, the matter has been stuck for several years with no party willing to budge on its own, and that's why judicial orders become the sole driving force in contracts between the warring public and

the most preferred mode of transportation, being able to handle very large consignments at low operation cost.

Since the mid-19th century, railways has been functioning in India and the British had laid the foundation network to take advantage of better connectivity through railways in administering India, and thereby controlling the people. Post-independence, the role of railways has expanded exponentially with many more routes being opened up and efforts being made to incorporate the cutting-edge rail technology in day-to-day working. This endeavour poses serious challenges in creation of suitable infrastructure to match the demands, which can only be met by bringing together public and private efforts. Thus, PPP is integral to the continuing development of railways in India.

Indian Railway Stations Development Corporation Ltd

The role of PPP is most evident in the development of railway stations in India with the setting up of the Indian Railway Stations Development Corporation (IRSDC) in 2012 as a special purpose vehicle (SPV) primarily for leapfrogging the stone-aged railway stations to modern avatars. This has been a long-pending demand of the population which could not be given due attention by different governments—Indian Railways is under the command and control of the central government—basically due to paucity of resources and the tussle between the local governments, central government and railway authorities as the main issue is of new use of the land with the Indian Railways. It is very well known that the Indian Railways has in its possession huge tracts of land around the existing railway stations and along the railway tracks all over the country.

Very often, the land lies either unused or grossly underused. Commercial exploitation of this valuable resource can do wonders both for the Indian Railways and for the population; however, the challenge is to opt for sustainable use and prevent the encroachment by land mafia. It is practically a very difficult task and simply cannot be done by local authorities only. Legal issues regarding rights for land usage and adverse possession (entitled due to long uninterrupted use) create problems of court proceedings and cases pending for decades without any effective legal remedy. The answer to such a problem is only through policy formulation and thereafter implementation at the highest level, bringing in together all the stakeholders and making the plan so that it is a win-win situation for everyone.

It is only possible when the size of the cake becomes large enough for all the stakeholders to get a sufficiently thick slice, and that can only be done when new commercial activities are allowed to take place at the existing railway stations by making them better places for the public to commute and transact. It can also be done at the places where there are no railway stations; however, the expansion of cities and semi-urban areas require new railway hubs for catering to the large population settled in these places, and still settling by finding new revenues for employment and residence.

The IRSDC has been given the mandate to take up projects for these purposes and act in an autonomous manner following the latest technology and principles of management, without any interference from the government and railway authorities. It has been given the responsibility, and also authority, to get the work done through PPP projects on the basis of build–operate–transfer (BOT), build–own–operate–transfer (BOOT), build–lease–transfer (BLT), etc., according

separate arrival and departure areas at railway stations which are extremely crowded presently. This may not be so easy to be done practically as a train, unlike an aircraft, stops at several railway stations en route to its final destination, and at every stop passengers alight and board at the same time. To make the problem more complex, there are multiple entry points to a train with several bogies.

Rather than letting the passengers wait for the train at the platform, there is a plan to make the passengers wait at the forecourt or concourse of the railway station making it a little bit more time taking for the passenger to reach the platform when the train arrives and thereafter board it. Gone will be the days when passengers can really sprint and board a train while it is steaming off the platform, and obviously the romanticism of Howrah Railway Station where the passengers were even allowed to take their car on the railway platform will be gone forever.

Keeping the target of the financial year 2018–2019 and the Lok Sabha elections in May 2019 in mind, there was a concerted effort by the Indian Railways to complete the revamping of at least four stations by the end of March 2019, and they were Gandhinagar, Habibganj, Charbagh and Gomti Nagar. The other three stations in advanced stage of redevelopment are Anand Vihar, Bijwasan and Chandigarh.[7] All this has been made possible because of the decision by the government in September–October 2018 to allow private parties to participate in the process of revamping of railway stations under

---

[7] Faizan Haidar, 'Railways to Redevelop 50 Stations at ₹7500 Crore', *The Hindustan Times*, 13 February 2019. Available at https://www.hindustantimes.com/india-news/railways-to-redevelop-50-stations-at-rs-7500-crore/story-YXdY6Ib5DW5qw218YY3zzI.html (accessed on 24 April 2019).

the control of nodal executing agency IRSDC. The lease term for contracts shall be 99 years, which may vary from project to project, as the market conditions and commercial viability of any specific project usually differ from any other project.

One-size-fits-all generally does not work in PPP project planning and execution. Flexibility is the key and, hence, the IRSDC may decide to have a cluster of railway stations rather than one, and multiple subleases if the developers are more comfortable with this idea, and if it also makes sense practically to follow it for a particular specific project. The control and coordination of the entire revamping exercise has been given to the IRSDC after experiencing the failure of the 'Swiss challenge' method[8] which entails an unsolicited offer by a developer with typically set procedure of inviting third parties to make better offers; and after receiving all the offers awarding the contract to the lowest bidder.

This has utterly failed as it is often very difficult for the developers to understand the big picture of the needs and aspirations of the people and the immediate demands of the contracting authority. In other words, it can be said to be encouraging ad hoc practices which may not fit together to complete the picture. Like a jigsaw puzzle with several parts, Swiss challenge has been, by definition, a microscopic view of the big problem and can only work fruitfully if the control is with a certain central and nodal authority.

Habibganj in Madhya Pradesh is the first railway station in India to be redeveloped. It is being done on the lines

---

[8] FE Bureau, 'Modi-Led Cabinet's Big Decision for Indian Railways! Stations to Be Redeveloped on PPP Model with Many Passenger Amenities,' *The Financial Express*, 4 October 2018. Available at https://www.financialexpress.com/infrastructure/railways/green-signal-modi-government-gives-nod-to-railway-station-revamp-programme/1336337/ (accessed on 24 April 2019).

Alstom was also aggrieved by the tender process and had challenged it in the Delhi High Court. Both the petitions—filed by Siemens and Alstom—were dismissed. Against that order, Siemens appealed in the Supreme Court, whereas Alstom preferred not to appeal. Siemens main ground in appeal had been that the GEC values were not sacrosanct and for international players in the market—the other competitors—it was quite possible to comment seriously about the achievability of the values. Siemens was of the view that the values offered by HR were not sustainable and, hence, the contract could not be awarded to HR, as there were very serious doubts about the viability of the project and enforcement of the contract, in the form it had been put forth by the bidder HR.

To support its stand, Siemens filed reports and views of committee of experts and of the concerned ministry that the values used by HR were not defensible. It was, therefore, urged by Siemens to award the contract to the lowest bidder, L1, according to price bid, that is, Siemens itself. Delhi Metro argued that multiple committees and subcommittees of experts had concluded that the GEC values were critical in deciding the L1, which cannot simply be on the basis of price bid and, hence, the award of contract on the basis of price bid along with GEC values was the right method to be followed.

There was also a penal provision in case the committed GEC values were not achieved by the contractors; hence, there was no convincing reason that the bidders would have used any arbitrary value for GEC while submitting their bids. There were issues raised regarding interference in the matter during its pendency in the court by the government, which would have made the functioning of Delhi Metro as an autonomous body a mere formality and also the process of law being hindered by administrative interventions. It was also contended that any judicial decision against the award of the contract to HR would have been against public interest and the commercial interest of the party in forcing the contract, that is, HR. Interesting observations, which are settled principles of law, were made by different counsel for different parties to the dispute, each relying on the well-established canons by taking the moral high ground.

Some of them were: role of courts is extremely limited in contracts and tendering process; staying the performance of a contract on the ground that the contract had been awarded wrongly must be done with highest levels of due diligence and circumspection; the process of award of public contracts, especially government contracts, should be transparent, equitable and capable of fixing accountability; the government or any other authority should not try to usurp the powers of the courts on any occasion and particularly when any matter is sub judice, etc. In this case, the high court had concluded that there was no irregularity in the process of awarding the contract.

The only ground on which Siemens had challenged this decision, and that too very assertively, is that Delhi Metro should have ascertained whether the GEC values as offered by the bidders were achievable or not. Besides this, Siemens did not have any other valid ground on which the award of the contract to HR could have been challenged. The Supreme Court was supposed to decide this short question regarding the process of finally giving the contract to HR without duly checking the attainability of the GEC value. Interesting question arises as to the feasibility of checking it by Delhi Metro, and whether it was possible in a reasonable manner or not. Moreover, it was also to be seen whether going through this rigmarole was at all necessary or sheer waste of time for a public entity like Delhi Metro which is working on a tight budget and rigid timelines.

Once an undertaking is given by a bidder regarding the values, which are quite scientific in nature and can only be scrutinized and approved by scientific experts in that particular domain, it is quite logical and rational that those values are accepted on the face, and with a penal provision for not adhering to the values, it surely makes sense to simply go ahead with finalization of awarding the contract and thereafter its execution. To strengthen its position, Delhi Metro had conducted a simulation exercise by which it was decided that the values mentioned by the bidders were not unachievable; however, it could not have been stated with full certainty, though there

The route of PPP was, therefore, the obvious method to upgrade the facilities at the airports. The AAI had achieved moderate success with the modernization of the Delhi and Mumbai airports through the PPP model in the early years of this century when there was sudden spurt in PPP, and it was seen as the solution for the long-time pending serious issues of non-development of facilities.

However, there had been numerous challenges in that process especially related to contractual breaches, and at times, failure to anticipate the heavy growth of air traffic along with the need to holistically view different activities necessary for success of business of airlines and benefits to the passengers. Air travel can be a real pleasure if the airports are lively, convenient to the passengers and also affordable. It is a real challenge for any organization developing airports to have global standards achieved with a shoestring budget. Even in the initial stage if sufficient amount of resources are made available, there is typically the problem of high-cost maintenance and somehow getting proper cash flow for meeting the day-to-day expenditure for the upkeep.

As the aspirations of most of the passengers travelling abroad, and having experienced really world-class airports, are quite high, it is extremely difficult to please them. Many a time airport modernization is understood only to make cosmetic changes with very heavy expenditure done on the façade of a building, murals, carpets, paintings, chandeliers, metal pots, luxurious furniture, etc. This is, truly speaking, not required for making a wonderful airport. The first and foremost person to be targeted in this entire exercise is the passenger. In the list of priority for passenger, safety comes first followed by convenience, and luxury is somewhere at the bottom. It is, however, quite natural that with adequate amount of resources made available, and sometimes a little more than needed, there is a tendency to splurge on unnecessary items and activities.

This has been very often observed at the airports maintained by the AAI, with every good thing made available for the so-called very important person (VIPs), whereas for the regular passengers scarcity of resources is pretty conspicuous. With the use of PPP model, there has been an effort to make things better for the ordinary routine passengers so that they can at least have some succour at the airport, while going through the anxiety and the uncertainty associated with any travel, especially air travel. With increase in air travel in non-metro cities in India, there had been an urgent need to upgrade the airports in these cities which were several decades old and could, at best, be said to be merely functional and that too only for old-styled aircraft with just basic infrastructure available.

With the purpose of modernizing the six airports at Guwahati, Thiruvananthapuram, Lucknow, Mangaluru, Ahmedabad and Jaipur, the Airports Economic Regulatory Authority (AERA) initiated the bidding process under the PPP model in late 2018.[11] Several private players submitted their bids and with the two-stage process of technical bidding and financial bidding, it is expected that successful bidders would find it financially viable to take up the projects. Interestingly, the concession period has been made 50 years with noticeable deviation from revenue sharing model as used in the Delhi and Mumbai airports. One of the important criteria in

---

[11] Saurabh Sinha, 'Privatisation: GMR, Adani Bid for All 6 AAI Airports,' *The Times of India*, 17 February 2019. Available at http://timesofindia.indiatimes.com/articleshow/68026906.cms?utm_source <hig>=</hig> contentofinterest&utm medium <hig>=</hig> text&utm_campaign <hig>=</hig> cppst (accessed on 24 April 2019).

selecting the right bid would be the 'per-passenger fee' in the new CAs for the six cities.

There had been serious allegations earlier against the private operators of separating certain non-core activities at the airports and assigning them to subsidiary companies by hiving them off to avoid sharing the revenue with the public entity. The 'per-passenger' formula, hopefully, will take care of this problem. All these are brownfield projects and even in some greenfield projects the per passenger formula will be used to test the real efficacy of revenue sharing in the long run. Interestingly, there had been waxing and waning of interest of bidders in the projects, which is a reflection of high levels of uncertainty in continuation of policy, roll-out and execution in the near future due to turbulence in market and political persistence. A pre-bid conference has been a good way of allaying the fears of bidders and signalling consistency and doggedness of the AAI in pursuing the modernization exercise with private participation.

CASE STUDY

DIAL v. International Lease Finance Corporation, Supreme Court of India, 2015[12]

Delhi International Airport Limited (DIAL), a joint venture (JV) based on PPP model, was granted aerodrome licence 2008 by the Directorate General of Civil Aviation (DGCA) for the functioning of the Delhi Airport. Under the AAI Act, 1994, DIAL was authorized to collect several fees from the airlines

---

[12] *Delhi International Airport Limited v. International Lease Finance Corporation and others*; Supreme Court of India; Bench: R. Banumathi, V. Gopala Gowda, JJ.; Reported in 2015 Indlaw SC 195; (2015) 8 SCC 446; AIR 2015 SC 1903; Date of decision: 17 March 2015; C.A. No. 2932 of 2015 (Arising out of S.L.P. (Civil) No. 27062/2013).

for the usage of the airport. International Lease Finance Corporation (ILFC)—not to be confused with the Indian company Infrastructure Leasing & Financial Services (IL&FS)—an American company earlier headquartered in California has been a major lessor of aircraft to different airlines globally. The Kingfisher Airlines (Kingfisher) headed by its flamboyant boss Vijay Mallya was not doing well and did not make timely payment to airport authorities.

Due to non-payment of fees, its airline licence was suspended and aircraft leased by the ILFC to Kingfisher were detained and deregistered, which clearly meant that the airlines could not fly the aircraft and deregistration meant that the aircraft was rendered simply a piece of metal without any legal permission to fly. For any aircraft leasing company, this is a huge loss as its resources are lying unused, and obviously with the passage of time the aircraft would require regular maintenance to be kept fit to be in a position to fly any moment. This is incurring extra expenditure without any revenue generation. For Kingfisher, things were already in bad shape and services were suspended so there was no real purpose to detain the aircraft; however, DIAL did not allow the aircraft to be returned to the lessor.

As Kingfisher was already moving on the path of bankruptcy, it was strategically in the ILFC's interest to get its aircraft back at the earliest. Thus, the real legal fight was between DIAL and ILFC for non-payment of airport fees by Kingfisher. The ILFC's aircraft were also detained by the AAI at numerous airports in the country, and Mumbai International Airport Limited (MIAL). Against this action, the ILFC had moved the Delhi High Court. In the meanwhile, negotiations were held between different parties for finding an amicable solution. One of the most important decisions made by the parties was that the airport authorities agreed to release the deregistered aircraft. On the basis of this decision, the Delhi High Court directed the release of the aircraft according to the conditions of the settlement.

Surprisingly, DIAL challenged the Delhi High Court direction by appealing to the Supreme Court on the ground that the meeting between the parties held earlier, and which formed the basis of the Delhi High Court direction, was only an executive decision which curtailed the statutory powers exercised by DIAL under the PPP model. Thus, the argument was that the minutes of meeting of the multi-party meeting did not have any statutory force, or the authority and sanctity of the central government order and, hence, it was not proper to rely on those minutes for obliging the airport authorities to release the aircraft by a judicial order. Earlier decisions were cited to support the point that executive orders can neither override nor amend statutory provisions.

Different charges are determined by the AERA—a statutory body constituted under the Airports Economic Regulatory Authority of India Act, 2008 (AERAI Act, 2008), and obviously none of regulations or rules can be inconsistent with the provisions of the AERAI Act, 2008, or the AAI Act, 1994, or any other law. The AAI had notified certain regulations, the Airport Authority of India (Management of Airports) Regulations, 2003, as empowered by the 1994 Act. Regulation 10 is under scrutiny:

> 10. Unless otherwise provided under the Act or by a general or special order in writing by the Central Government, the use of the movement area of Airport, by an aircraft shall be subject to payment of such landing, parking or housing fees or charges as are levied by the Authority from time to time. In the event of non-payment of the requisite fee or charges, the Competent Authority shall have a right to detain or stop departure of the aircraft till the fees or charges are paid to Authority, which may include the current and accumulated dues.

The competent authority in the instant case is DIAL, and there is no dispute about it between the parties. Hence, DIAL had claimed that it had full authority to detain the aircraft. However, the central government asserted that it had made the decision, as mentioned in the minutes of the meeting and, therefore, it should be considered to be an exception, and that too in writing, as mentioned in the opening words of regulation 10.

Commenting on the approach taken by the Delhi High Court, the Supreme Court observed that the high court had not gone into the legality and sustainability of the minutes according to neither the provisions of the AAI Act nor the regulations. Thus, the Supreme Court took on itself to go into the detailed analysis of the questions involved about the order. After discussing the constitutional scheme of things about how the central government and state governments should conduct business, the Supreme Court observed that the minutes of the meeting were not sanctioned or sanctified by the cabinet or the concerned ministries. Thus, the minutes could not be deemed to be an order by the central government in writing, which in turn meant that the action taken by DIAL was upheld by the Supreme Court, and the decision of the Delhi High Court directing release of the aircraft quashed.

This final decision was made despite DIAL being a party to the meeting where it had agreed to the terms and conditions of the settlement giving a very strong message that while dealing with the government, one has to be extremely careful about the legalities and the procedural compliance. It is also quite surprising that the central government, if it really wanted the aircraft to be released, did not pay sufficient attention to the finer aspects of sanctification by the concerned ministries and departments. It is even more surprising when one brings into consideration the fact that the army of bureaucrats and ministerial staff in any ministry and department is well adept with the procedural aspects and, on most of the occasions, style takes precedence over substance, that is, procedural law does become more important than substantive law.

There can be another view; however, the possibility is dim. To keep the various parties involved in the dispute in good humour, it might have been deliberately done by the central government delegation. It is difficult to accept the fact that not getting the minutes of the meeting sanctified to give them legal validity was an oversight, or simply ignorance of the procedure. The PPP model with international and domestic business players involved is also under the scrutiny of other foreign investors. Also, international treaties obligate India, as a signatory, to act fairly and provide a level playing field to foreign investors and businesses doing business in India.

Certain international aviation treaty—Cape Town Convention and Protocol[13]—was also used by the central government as a defence tool to get the decision, as mentioned in the minutes of the meeting, enforced. It also speaks volumes about the lack of attention paid to the minutes, when these were directly related to an international convention. Expectedly, there should have been extra care taken and attention paid to ensure enforcement of the minutes to be on the safe side. The uncertainty in dealing with the government in any contract is usually of a highly variable nature, depending on the context; governments may change and reverse the policies, or the same government may think in a different manner with the passage of time and change the contractual terms to suit its convenience.

It is true that uncertainties cannot be eliminated in a contract; however, contracts between private parties are usually guided by mutual benefits, and parties are usually willing to negotiate to a certain extent if things unfold in a manner different than envisaged. But, in a PPP CA, the parties involved are typically private and government on one side, as one single entity, dealing with other parties. Rules of the game do not remain the same as constitutional obligations, read in fine print and administrative rigmarole have to be taken care of. There is no escape from them. The minutes, in the instant case, did not result in a final decision as understood in the terms of the Constitution of India and, hence, the decisions taken in the meeting were of no value for all practical purposes.

Intervention by the governments of the day in the functioning of otherwise autonomous organizations creates problems and takes away all the freedom and authority given to them for exercise in day-to-day activities and also in planning and strategizing. A JV in the form of a PPP must have the necessary

---

[13] Convention on International Interests in Mobile Equipment, 2001. India became signatory to this convention in 2008.

independence in functioning, otherwise there remains no difference between the government, that is, public entities, and private organizations. It is heartening that the Supreme Court decided in favour of the JV—DIAL, though on strictly legal technicality, and thereby vindicating the independence of the PPP from the government. Practically, it is quite difficult in routine functioning to insulate the PPP entities form governmental indirect control and pressures.

RIVERS AND SEA PORTS

India is a land of rivers and also has a very large coastline. Both these water bodies have not been fully used for transportation purposes. The rivers are used very little, or for all practical purposes they remain unused when compared to rivers in other parts of the developed world, for passenger and cargo movement. Wherever they are being used, the methods are traditional and rudimentary. Boats and ferries need modernization to be safe, comfortable and energy efficient. The river banks and docks have degraded excessively because of unregulated erosion and pollution. Natural harbours on the sea coasts have also been under unimaginable ruination over decades primarily due to uncontrolled commercial exploitation coupled with lack of administrative intent to maintain them. The world in the meanwhile has moved several decades ahead with technology and new management techniques transforming shipping and river transport. To catch with the world, we in India have to move quite fast, both in policy formulation and implementation. Substantive portion of international trade depends on shipping and India can do well to exploit its large coastline fully by making sea ports of global standards and by providing updated facilities at its various ports.

Major Port Trusts: Stressed PPP projects

There have been serious problems with the PPP projects at the major ports basically due to very high storage charges. The competition with the private ports has been tough, which usually offer free storage period for long durations, taking away a lot of business from the ports managed under the PPP projects. Non-usage of the facilities at these ports results in underutilization of the berth. Clearing of cargo at ports in India takes a much longer time as compared with the major popular ports all over the world. It is not as if the infrastructure is absent in every port in India; however, it is quite certain that the willingness to take risks in providing the world-class services is truly missing, which makes the ports' maintenance heavily dependent on the whims and fancies of a few individuals manning the show.

Also, the delay caused in transacting business at the ports results in loss of revenue and missing several otherwise good opportunities. To resolve these issues, the Ministry of Shipping in India made certain changes in 2018.[14] There are different stages of delay and within a certain period—known as free period—no storage charge is to be levied. If the delay is more than five days, but within the extended free period, the PPP operator is obliged to pay the port trust 1 per cent of the annual revenue requirement (ARR). After the extended free period, the PPP operator is supposed to pay actual storage charges or the 1 per cent of ARR, whichever is higher.

A stressed PPP is not able to meet the business target as envisaged in the annual business plan, due to a variety of reasons,

---

[14] P. Manoj, 'Shipping Ministry Clears Bail-Out Plan for Stressed PPP Projects at Major Ports,' *BusinessLine*, 4 September 2018. Available at https://www.thehindubusinessline.com/economy/logistics/shipping-ministry-clears-bail-out-plan-for-stressed-ppp-projects-at-major-ports/article24865796.ece (accessed on 24 April 2019).

however, the fact of the matter is that the port operators due to higher costs and specialized nature find it difficult to make profit. The workload at any port is anticipated for a particular year and efforts are made to get a realistic number based on experience and market conditions. It is quite obvious that many a time the projected target is not able to be achieved, but too much shortfall is surely troublesome, and the administration at any port is supposed to find suitable answers for the gap. Certain objective criteria have been made. Broadly, these set the bar; however, these cannot be applied mechanically.

At best, these can be taken as some indicative numbers, with the final decision making power of declaring a port as stressed or not with the competent authorities. For instance, less than 70 per cent of the target achieved, incurring losses to reduce its market value by half, etc., are some of the criteria. Heavy control by the government in ports managed on the PPP model have not been giving commercial returns, though strategically it is important for the government to have an upper hand in port management, at least at the policymaking level. Ports provide an easy ingress and egress both for goods and persons, whether done legally or illegally. Bringing in goods illegally from foreign lands or letting goods leave Indian shores without proper legal approval results in smuggling of goods, which is a threat for the country's economy and security.

Human trafficking is also a possibility from unregulated or leniently regulated ports. Thus, it is not always due to poor application of management concepts and inadequate infrastructure that delays happen at major ports in India. Safety and security come first and can never be compromised for commercial reasons. Still, there are certain areas of work which require tightening and using better management techniques to achieve the set targets annually. Sometimes tweaking the policy a little bit and thereafter modifying rules and regulations works. It requires allowing re-negotiating CAs for managing the ports.

When it becomes a question of survival of the port's business, it is desirable, but there is a catch. In the hope of getting an already ongoing CA changed in one's favour, some operators let the things go down the slope to reach the stage of being declared as 'stressed,' which simply defeats the very purpose of bringing in private players to the ports. Early in 2018, the government had worked on the genuine problems faced by the private port operators for a long time and had tried to make it more investor friendly. One important change was made by providing exit option to the operators after two years of operation, which had already been a provision in the Highway sector.

Major Ports PPP: Model Concession Agreement and Tariff Authority for Major Ports

The law in India for the major ports—very big ports; other ports are minor ports and intermediate ports—is the Major Port Trusts Act, 1963. There are 13 major ports in India: Kolkata Port, Paradip Port, New Mangalore Port, Cochin Port, Jawaharlal Nehru Port, Mumbai Port, Kandla Port, Vishakhapatnam Port, Chennai Port, Tuticorin Port, Ennore Port, Mormugao Port and Port Blair Port. There are concerns about their management and making the optimal use of the available resources. Private participation in the form of PPP does help in making things work more effectively than relying solely on government, whether central or state. Tariff regulation at the major ports is done by an independent authority, The Tariff Authority for Major Ports (TAMP), constituted in 1997 by amending the Major Port Trusts Act, 1963.

The TAMP is mandated to regulate all the tariffs related to vessel, cargo, lease of properties at the major ports, etc. Its functioning has to be within the framework created by the Major Port Trusts Act, 1963. As heavy stakes are involved in shipping, and tariffs and charges can be quite high, many disputes arise resulting in time-taking litigation and other adjudicatory processes. To simplify the matters and make the PPPs more lucrative for private players, the revised model concession agreement (MCA) provided for the exit clause after two years as mentioned earlier. Also, the land rent for concessionaire was reduced. Royalty payment by the concessionaire has been modified to make it more practical and investor friendly. It had been a highly contentious issue with many projects suffering due to wrong application of formula for royalty determination.

More independence had been given to concessionaire for using better technology and modern equipment. It is a little bit surprising that any such constraint—of not using the latest techniques without approval—should have any place in the MCA. Measures had been taken to make project's cost more realistic and closer to the actual numbers, rather than sticking to some numbers estimated in the beginning. There had been extremely painful situations for concessionaires due to the 'force majeure' clause. Usually, the parties to a CA find it highly contentious to agree to a commonly understood meaning of the phrase force majeure. One of the most disputed reasons is 'change in law', which is possible either due to legislative change, or by an executive order, or by a new interpretation by the court of law.

In any such instance, the parties always try to have the interpretation done as convenient to them at that time. To avoid such possibilities, the CAs were revised to have detailed meaning of 'change in law' including new TAMP orders and guidelines, change in taxes, environment law, labour law, etc., which would be pertinent to the operations conducted by the concessionaire. The technicality of the date on which the operations were deemed to commence formally and, in the legal sense, called as the commercial operation date (COD) was an issue as practically things usually start either earlier or later than date. Making the facilities available to the concessionaire and allowing the commencement of operations even before the COD had been permitted in revised MCA.

Refinancing at low cost had been facilitated for making projects financially viable. Reducing disputes and resolving disputes speedily is necessary for ports and, hence, the experience of dispute redressal in highways in the form of Society for Affordable Redressal of Disputes (SAROD) had been used for ports also. Filing complaints and monitoring had been made simpler.[15] The confidence of concessionaires by providing the options of working together with the concessioning authority to make the projects successful has been boosted. The earlier attitude of the parties of 'us' versus 'them', as concessionaire versus port authority, did not help the creation of positive working environment at the ports and business did not grow as was expected.

With changes in the circumstances due to various reasons—global shipping business is impacted hugely by policy decisions of the big shipping nations and tariff wars between the shipping superpowers—private players, as parties to CAs, have very little say and freedom in operating. The position of these port operators is quite risky. Moreover, with the PPP

---

[15] *Business Standard*, 'Government Revises Model Concession Agreement for PPP in Major Ports,' 9 March 2018. Available at https://www.business-standard.com/article/news-cm/government-revises-model-concession-agreement-for-ppp-in-major-ports-118030900521_1.html (accessed on 24 April 2019).

projects to be very well defined and under the ambit of constitutional provisions of following all the fundamental rights, especially right to equality and being treated fairly, and the right to information and media glare, the private players in the PPP projects find themselves in the unenvious position of being a private player and still carrying the burden of State.

CASE STUDY

JSW Infrastructure v. Kakinada Seaports, Supreme Court of India, 2017[16]

Paradip port in the state of Odisha is a major port of India. The Paradip Port Trust wanted to mechanize the East Quay berths for better utilization of resources and to increase the efficiency of working. For this purpose, it issued the request for qualification (RfQ) from global players. As a PPP project, it was on BOT basis for a concession period of 30 years. Four parties submitted RFQ. They all qualified for the next stage of RfP. Only two submitted their bids. The first consortium was of JSW Infrastructure and South West Port, and the second consortium was of Kakinada Seaports, Bothra Shipping and MBG Commodities.

The first consortium's (hereinafter JSW) bid was higher as compared to the second consortium's (hereinafter Kakinada) bid and, hence, JSW's bid was to be accepted. However, Kakinada objected it on the ground that the port's policy did not allow creation of monopoly and, JSW was already operating one berth. Despite the objection, the concession was

---

[16] *JSW Infrastructure Limited and another v. Kakinada Seaports Limited and others;* Supreme Court of India; 1 March 2017; Civil Appeal No. 3422 of 2017 (Arising out of Special Leave Petition (Civil) No. 23241 of 2016), Civil Appeal No. 3424 of 2017 (Arising out of Special Leave Petition (Civil) No. 23695 of 2016); Bench: D. P. Gupta, Madan B. Lokur, JJ.; Reported in 2017 Indlaw SC 175; AIR 2017 SC 1175; 2017 (121) ALR 867; JT 2017 (3) SC 77; 2017(3) SCALE 216.

awarded to JSW. Kakinada moved the Orissa High Court against the award of concession to JSW. The main ground was that the policy did not allow a private operator already operating a berth to bid for the next berth. The policy clause which Kakinada relied on is reproduced.

> Policy Clause: If there is only one private terminal/berth operator in a port for a specific cargo, the operator of that berth or his associates shall not be allowed to bid for the next terminal/berth for handling the same cargo in the same port.

Kakinada relied heavily on the fact that JSW was operating berth for dry cargo, and the berth to be built under the PPP was also for dry cargo, hence submission of bid by JSW was in violation of the policy clause. What could have been the interpretation of the word 'next' used in the policy clause was to be decided by the Orissa High Court. It interpreted that the word 'next' meant that a private operator was not supposed to bid for the next successive berth. It was, however, qualified with the condition that the next berth should be for the same type of cargo—containers, liquid, dry bulk, etc.—as the previous berth to bar the operator of the existing berth to participate in the bidding process. In the instant case, cargo for both the berths—existing and the one to be built—was dry cargo.

It was, therefore, held by the high court that JSW's bid was wrongly considered. After coming to this conclusion, the high court set aside the award of concession to JSW. It directed the Paradip Port Trust to award the concession to Kakinada if it was willing to match the financial bid of JSW or go ahead with fresh bidding process. In any case, despite being the successful bidder, JSW was neither to be awarded the concession nor to be considered in the fresh bidding process. Thus, JSW was aggrieved. Also, Paradip Port Trust was aggrieved as the entire bidding process had to be carried out again, or the second best bidder had to be awarded the concession. Both were not the ideal and desirable scenarios.

Both JSW and Paradip appealed in the Supreme Court. The argument made by JSW was that the word next had to be interpreted according to the context and intention of the framers of the policy which primarily was to avoid creation of monopolies, obviously to infuse competition in the system, and hence it is important to understand the reference in which an existing operator was not allowed to bid. The contention was that it was only if one operator was managing the affairs for a particular type of cargo, then that operator would not be allowed to do that; however, when there are number of operators already operating and managing different berths, then the meaning of next should not be to restrain an existing operator.

However, Kakinada argued that interpretation should be only to the plain and simple meaning as understood from the literal reading of the text, which undoubtedly means the next successive berth which clearly disqualifies JSW from bidding. Factually, there were more than one operators handling dry cargo and thus there was no possibility of one party becoming a monopoly in a particular type of cargo handling. The Supreme Court held that the Orissa High Court did not take into consideration the opening words of the policy clause, '...If there is only one private terminal/berth operator in a port for a specific cargo...', and thus its decision was erroneous and could not be upheld. Kakinada lost the case in the Supreme Court and the decision was in favour of Paradip Port Trust and JSW.

The Supreme Court, while making this decision, cited liberally from one of the landmark judgement on administrative law and awarding of contracts—*Ramana Dayaram Shetty v. International Airport Authority of India*[17]—and observed that words in a document cannot be treated as superfluous. It is interesting to note that for the interpretation of the word 'next', the matter had been litigated till the Supreme Court. Was it such a difficult thing to be done by the parties involved or for the high court? It can easily be understood that the purpose of Kakinada, or for that matter any losing party in a

---

[17] (1979) 3 SCC 489; 1979 Indlaw SC 16.

CA, is not to allow the winning party in the tender procedure to enjoy the fruit of its labour peacefully.

Such is the judicial procedure and complexity of the wide network of substantive law that the losing party usually finds one pretext or the other to challenge the award of any contract. The role of the State and the government have been widely explained and interpreted minutely in hundreds of cases in the high courts and the Supreme Court. The Shetty case is one of the landmark judgements on this issue and can undoubtedly be said to be like the authority on such matters. No serious case in a court of law related to award of a government contract, especially of very high stakes, is ever decided without making a reference to the Shetty case.

Though the JSW–Kakinada case was decided in the Supreme Court on the narrow issue of interpretation of the word 'next', the larger picture is important to be seen and appreciated. The main concern was not of interpretation, but that of using the available resources optimally, and also to encourage private participation. The policy clause is itself contradictory to a certain extent. Why should the policy be made in such a manner that existing private operators find themselves at a disadvantage while applying for additional work in the same organization? It does not make sense.

The only argument presented to support this narrow view is that monopoly is bad for any business and, hence, the public sector or the State cannot encourage more business being cornered by one single entity even if it is quite in alignment with the management thinking of economies of scale and letting the private player develop symbiotic relationship in the business. Also, if one big player handles many operations of the same kind, the overhead costs are reduced. This is the ingenuity and innovativeness of the specific private player, and for this reason precisely this private player must be encouraged to do more of the work of the same nature. But, the policy is exactly otherwise making it difficult for any private operator to scale up the business and make reasonable profits by cutting the common cost, and also by learning from the mistakes previously committed.

For such large projects, it is difficult to even get other private players who can give real and fierce competition to the existing players. Simply for the sake of paperwork to justify the award of CA to the highest or lowest bidder, depending on the nature of project, there may be more than one party willing to submit its bid, but completing any such big project is not easy even for most of the well-established players in the market. It truly makes sense to allow the existing players with tremendous experience to take up the new work available and only in case the terms and condition of the existing players just do not match with that of the port trusts, there can be invitation given to new players.

But, this is a policy decision, which is to be made at the very top keeping in mind the directions given by the central government, global best practices which are often not followed, exigencies and urgency of the project. Very often, the urgency shown on the completion of projects leaves much to be desired as experienced and qualified persons are not allowed to create a caucus and take the entire business of ports in their hands. To a certain extent, this is desirable in India, with a major chunk of the population, and especially the well-trained technocrats, needs to be guided by the statutorily mentioned CAs and lawyers. The compliance report at various milestones achieved and after routine period of time gives a good reflection of the planned work and the work finally completed. Keeping the private operators quite tight does not allow them to become complacent and spread mediocrity in the performance.

POWER

In the growing age of industrialization and heavy demand for power also for household use, power sector has been at the forefront of receiving importance in policy formulation and execution; however, the role of private sector has conspicuously gained prominence in the last couple of decades only. The shift of the country towards open economy, from a closed economy, in the early 1990s has seen private participation increasing rapidly. Power generation, transmission and distribution (T&D), all have active private business participation, with control by statutory and regulatory bodies. Often, there are issues of balancing the demands of the private players, consumers and the government, which are being handled with growing maturity by power regulators and courts.

As the trends are changing to adopt more renewable energy in everyday life, the power sector is witnessing a dramatic shift from thermal, hydro and nuclear to solar, wind, tidal and other forms of power generation. Even with all these changes, which make tremendous sense for the long-term benefits to the environment, there is still merit in continuing with the old and traditional way of generating power, which is thermal, by using coal, oil or gas. The demands are typically not met by renewable energy sources due to low supply, and in a fast developing country like India, until and unless the country decides to turn the clock back in the direction of basic and rural economy model, demand is not going to go down.

The Electricity Act, 2003

The Electricity Act, 2003, was enacted with the purpose of making an overall change in the power sector in the country. At that time, there was an urgent need to pay attention to extremely important issues involved in generation, distribution and transmission of power in India. By that time, a decade had passed since economic liberalization in 1991 and the private sector in the country had started enjoying the freedom of doing business in the country, especially in the infrastructure sector; however, they were often complaints about the sector being heavily regulated and controlled by the government. There was still a lot to be done to meet the demands of the private sector which was quite anxious to play the important role of transforming the sector to reach to its potential.

For a very long time since Independence of the country in 1947, the power sector in India had been a sort of monopoly of the government with the private sector playing an insignificant role. For the last almost five decades, the public sector had done a decent job; however, it could have surely done much better to rise to the expectations of the people. There were large number of stories about inefficiency, corruption, nepotism in this sector and, above all, setting very low targets for performance. Even these targets were not achieved by the public sector mostly due to unwillingness of the individuals in positions of power to take hard decisions, and also due to paucity of resources and inability to incorporate the latest technology and management techniques resulting in huge losses and non-delivery of uninterrupted and un-fluctuating power, both to industries and households.

The quality of power supply in terms of extreme fluctuations in voltage had been pathetic, and uninterrupted supply was almost unheard of in the entire country barring a few pockets of elitist sections of society, which were politically well-connected. Power theft was frequent which was often attributed to losses during transmission; however, most of these losses were truly speaking blatant power theft by unscrupulous and politically protected businesses. The earlier laws were found to be ineffective to control the corrupt and dishonest practices. These were the Indian Electricity Act, 1910, and the Electricity (Supply) Act, 1948, and the Electricity Regulatory Commissions Act, 1998.

Most of the activities regarding power generation, distribution and transmission were under the control of the state governments through state electricity boards, which were sort of autonomous bodies, but for all practical purposes were controlled by the state governments, which usually left no chance to milk them fully for their political advantage, without bothering about financial and technical viability of projects and awarding contracts. Power was heavily subsidized for households and in several states power was given almost for free to farmers and to take care of this subsidy power was sold at prohibitive rates to big industries—as small and medium-sized industries were also provided power at subsidized rates—making it extremely difficult financially for the industrial sector to depend on the state electricity boards for supply of power. It was absolutely unthinkable and unreasonable that even after paying such high rate, most of the industries were not sure about the uninterrupted supply of power at proper voltage.

The determination of tariff for power supply was, thus, mandated to independently created electricity regulatory commissions under the Electricity Regulatory Commissions Act, 1998. It was under this act that the Central Electricity Regulatory Commission (CERC) was created in 1998, and different states also created the State Electricity Regulatory Commissions (SERCs). Their role was primarily to rationalize the electricity tariffs and take care of the related activities by formulation of policies and other issues related to tariff regulation. The jurisdiction of the CERC and SERCs has been divided so that there is no confusion, but still on many occasions there are certain overlapping issues which require clarity and often matters are taken to judicial forums, including at the highest level of the Supreme Court of India, to get these issues resolved.

As the name suggests, regulating tariffs of central generating stations is within the purview of the CERC along with any of the operations related to interstate generation, T&D, whereas the SERCs are empowered to determine tariff for the state units and other issues related to intrastate activities. One of the important functions performed by these regulatory commissions is adjudication of disputes within their respective jurisdictions between the power companies to resolve disputes related to tariff fixation, decide matters related to several licenses and work towards the development of a fair, transparent and reliable power trading system. An Appellate Tribunal for Electricity (APTEL) has been created under the Electricity Act, 2003, to hear appeals challenging the decisions of the CERC and SERCs. It can also entertain original petitions according to the provisions of the Electricity Act, 2003.

Under the provisions of the Electricity (Supply) Act, 1948, the Central Electricity Authority (CEA) was constituted which later on was brought under the purview of Electricity Act, 2003, after the repeal of the 1948 law. The authority is the nodal body for policy matters and advises the government on policy and related issues. At the time of its formation in 1951, it used to function as a part-time body; however, it was made a full-time body in 1975, which was one of the most important years in the history of governance and administration in India; being the year when Emergency was imposed in the country by the then government headed by the then Prime Minister Indira Gandhi.

Mid-1970s was a turbulent period and the so-called Licence-Permit Raj was at its zenith making the availability of almost every resource, including power, for business and industrialization in short supply, even if it was possible to make it available in adequate quantity, if not in surplus. Power, for a long time, had been in short supply and primarily because of skewed policies for generation, T&D, neither the industries nor the households were getting sufficient power, which had pushed the country towards the Stone Age. It was necessary at that time to have a central body to prepare proper policies taking into account the views of all the stakeholders, particularly users, both industries and households, and also learning from the experience of developed and other developing countries.

It was of utmost importance at that time to have the eyes and ears open and take into account the views of academicians, researchers and critics, among others. It was very difficult in those days for anyone to give frank and candid opinion and criticize the policies and plans of the government due to heavy imposition of restrictions on free speech and even penalizing such persons directly or indirectly. Thus, it was next to impossible for any well-intentioned and sincere person to give honest opinion. It is not difficult to understand that the CEA did not do anything useful in the ensuing years since its formation and the hangover of remaining static and just pushing the files continued for decades, making this body of no real use.

With the new law enacted in 2003, CEA has been an active body with the principal task of standardization of construction of different units necessary for power, grids equipment and also taking into consideration the holistic picture of hydropower generation with use of water for drinking, irrigation etc. Thus, CEA is not only concerned with power in isolation but as a chief policymaking body is working towards standardization. It is taking care of a large number of linked issues, either making decisions directly which are under its mandate, or coordinating with other authorities and bodies to make the overall impact of policies on execution positive and meaningful in the long run. Technical standards have to be set for private and public players taking into consideration the requirements of the country and some of the special geographical and climatic conditions in different parts of the country.

One-size-fits-all approach can never be successful in India, a country of continental size dimensions with extreme variations in topography, soil conditions, rainfall, exposure to sun, wind conditions, snow, etc. Bringing in this diversity into decision-making and also the fact that the technological developments take place at a very rapid pace, a pace which is usually not possible for policymaking and standard-setting bodies, it is desirable that the companies, whether public or private, executing the projects for generation, transmission and distribution must be given the necessary freedom to operate without being burdened by avoidable constraints. Thus, in a sense it can be said that the standards set by CEA are recommendatory in nature and not mandatory for the executing companies. At times, there is a problem of the CEA standards being a little dated and conservative for a private company which would typically like to incorporate the latest in technology so as to achieve highest efficiency, effectiveness and thereby make maximum profit.

CEA has really worked well in providing proper power grids in different regions and also with neighbouring countries. It is supposed to be an expert technical body. In the changing world with less reliance on fossil fuel such as oil and coal, there is a shift towards clean electricity generated from wind or solar power. There has been in the recent past more decentralization regarding power generation, T&D. Smaller regions or political units of states are no more supposed to be viable models for power. It has been proved by experience, and facts and figures that larger units in terms of geographical area and power usage are better managed technically and financially. National power grid, rather than regional grids, is favoured, often linked to neighbouring power supplying or demanding countries.

CASE STUDY

Uttar Haryana Bijli Vitran Nigam v. Adani Power, Supreme Court of India, 2019[18]

Pursuant to the Electricity Act, 2003, the distribution of power was decentralized in most of the states and typically the bigger states were divided into north, south, east and west, and autonomous units created for this purpose. In the state of Haryana, the distribution companies for north and south were made and called Uttar Haryana Bijli Vitran Nigam Ltd and Dakshin Haryana Bijli Vitran Nigam Ltd. In the Hindi language, *Uttar* means north, and *Dakshin* means south. Collectively, we call them Haryana discoms, which had filed an appeal in the Supreme Court. Gujarat Urja Vikas Nigam Ltd (GUVNL) from the state of Gujarat had also filed an appeal, and both the appeals were heard together.

The pertinent facts start from the year 2005 when special economic zones (SEZs) were created under the SEZ Act, 2005. The developers of SEZs, which were private companies, were given certain exemptions in customs, excise, etc. Adani, a prominent business company in Gujarat, had been the co-developer of Mundra SEZ in the Kutch district of Gujarat. The GUVNL was granted approval by the Ministry of Commerce and Industry (Ministry) to set up a power plant in the SEZ. It did so and signed power purchase agreements (PPAs) with Adani. In 2015, the government withdrew the exemption of most of the duties, which hitherto were exempted. A year later, exemption from service tax was also withdrawn. Thus, it was double whammy for Adani. Facing the heat in business due to loss from withdrawal of exemptions, Adani moved the CERC to claim compensation for change in law according to the provisions of the PPA.

Article 13 of the PPA provided for 'change in law'. This is interesting that the law is dynamic in nature and may change

---

[18] *Uttar Haryana Bijli Vitran Nigam Limited [UHBVNL] and another v. Adani Power Limited and others*, Supreme Court of India, 25 February 2019; Bench: R. F. Nariman, Navin Sinha, JJ.; Reported in 2019 Indlaw SC 232; Civil Appeal No. 5865 of 2018 with Civil Appeal No. 6190 of 2018.

with the passage of time due to a variety of reasons. When parties enter into an agreement, they do so on the basis of the existing law and they try to make the best use of the legal provisions so as to consolidate their position in terms of making maximum profit or otherwise to achieve their goals. It is quite devastating for the parties to a contract to know that their winning pitch and clauses have become useless, not because of the change in the conduct of either of the parties to the contract, but due to the change in law, which ordinarily is not in the hands of the parties.

To mitigate the damage due to any change in law, parties may mention such clauses, which is dependent on the higher position of the parties on the learning curve. In case a party has burnt its fingers once due to change in law, it will be very cautious in any future contract and would like to hedge its risks by passing the burden onto the other party also. Until and unless one party is in a seriously dominating position vis-à-vis the other party, it is not possible for one part to the contract to have everything in its favour. The other party would surely like to strike a balance in the contract so that it is not lopsided.

Primarily, change in law included any change brought out by legislative action or interpretation of the black letter law, or any contractual clauses, by the courts of competent jurisdiction. Interestingly, Article 13 also included any substantial change in contractual clauses resulting in change in any cost or revenue in sale of power. It also provided the rationale for inclusion of this clause, which was to compensate the affected party to the same economic position if the law had not changed. This is the principle of restitution—making good the loss—incorporated in the PPA to take care of any occurrence of loss suffered by a party. Thus, the idea of restitution has been accepted by the parties at the stage of negotiating the contract and need to be addressed in case of any aggrieved party through the case facts and provisions of the clause in the PPA, rather than addressing it directly to the judicial forum in an unstructured manner.

The parties had agreed that the quantum of compensation, in any such case, shall be determined by the appropriate commission, and the commission's decision shall be final and binding; however, the decision can be appealed in the appellate body according to the provision of the law. The parties had also agreed to with respect to the procedure to be followed, adjustment of monthly tariff, etc., with the restitution period divided into two phases—construction period and operation period—with different rules of the game for compensation. The Supreme Court held that Adani was legally entitled according to the Article 13, as provided in the PPA, and not on the basis of equity or fairness. The APTEL had decided on the basis of Article 13, which was the correct approach taken and, therefore, there was no need for the Supreme Court to interfere with the challenged decision.

CASE STUDY

Energy Watchdog v. CERC

One interesting and important case cited and discussed in the Uttar Haryana Bijli Vitran case was that decided by the Supreme Court in 2017—*Energy Watchdog v. CERC*[19]—which inter alia was regarding the change in Indonesian law. It was because of the change in law in Indonesia that coal supplies from there to India had become financially unviable forcing the private power operators to plead for re-negotiation of CAs. But the Supreme Court held that change in foreign law would not be covered by any contractual clause giving protection—and thus making a provision for compensation—for the change in law. It is true that due regard must be given

---

[19] *Energy Watchdog and others v. Central Electricity Regulatory Commission and others*, Supreme Court of India, 11 April 2017; Bench: R. F. Nariman, Pinaki Chandra Ghose, JJ.; Reported in 2017 Indlaw SC 275; 2017 (3) AWC 2692; JT 2017 (6) SC 161; 2017(4) SCALE 580; (2017) 14 SCC 80; Civil Appeal Nos. 5399–5400 of 2016, Civil Appeal No. 5347 of 2016, Civil Appeal No. 5348 of 2016, Civil Appeal No. 5364 of 2016, Civil Appeal No. 5346 of 2016, Civil Appeal Nos. 5351–5352 of 2016, Civil Appeal No. 5415/2016, Civil Appeal Nos. 9635–9642 of 2016, Civil Appeal No. 9035 of 2014.

to the basic principle of restitution; however, when contractual clauses are in direct conflict with equity, and one of them must prevail, it is usually the contract which should be allowed to prevail, as that has been the mutual decision of the contractual parties, until and unless it results in something so absurd and unrealistic that the court decides that it could never have been the intention of the legislature or the parties to the agreement.

The price of Indonesian coal had gone up beyond the anticipation of the private power operators, but that could not be the basis of bringing any change in the PPAs using the 'doctrine of frustration', which makes it possible for a party to a contract not to perform its contractual obligations as it becomes impossible to be performed; however, impossibility must be due to certain unforeseen events, which typically does not include commercial difficulty, until and unless mentioned in the contract. In this case, it was nowhere mentioned in the contract that the coal had to be procured only from Indonesia, and that too at a certain price. It was undoubtedly a risk taken by the private power operators, which they had preferred to take willingly and after knowing all the terms and conditions of the agreements.

When they had agreed to provide power at a particular tariff, it became their contractual duty to do so, even if the input cost of coal had unexpectedly gone up. That is precisely the purpose of entering into a contract: to move from the zone of uncertainty to the zone of certainty. The contractual provisions were quite clear that the change in Indonesian law would not be included in the meaning of 'change in law' which was intended to mean only the change in Indian law. This decision came as a big disappointment to the private players as their hopes to get judicial remedy on the basis of provisions of contract, or even equity, were dashed by the Supreme Court.

It was not at all possible for the private companies as contractual parties to the PPAs to provide power at the tariff determined earlier and frozen by the power regulatory bodies. Commercial non-viability of any such project would have meant huge losses for the private operators, in case they had gone ahead to honour their word. But, private companies are doing business primarily to make a profit and not unnecessarily continue to supply power by making losses. Thus, the matter was again taken to the courts on the basis of changed scenario of doing business and on the central plank of 'public interest'. In October 2018, the Supreme Court had allowed re-negotiation of the PPAs and, therefore, amendments to be made subject to approval by the CERC.[20]

The consumer body, Energy Watchdog, was to be given a chance by the regulators to be heard as consumer interests would be negatively impacted by tariff rise; however, in the long run the consumers would suffer more if the units shut down. Thus, it had been a trade-off, not strictly in legal terms, but keeping in mind the long-term interests of the consumers and the economy. Re-negotiations between power operators and different state governments did not result in any immediate increase in tariff, but efforts have been and are being made to reach a balance between the interests of the consumers and service providers so as to have realistic changes.[21]

TELECOMMUNICATION

In the last two decades or so, one of the greatest impacts on the lives of the people has been due to rapid advancements in telecommunication. The mobile phone in the pockets of people has become increasingly powerful, with tremendous potential for empowering everyone in the farthest of the places from the centre of governance. Providing the requisite infrastructure to make it possible is the job of the governments;

---

[20] Priyanka Mittal, 'Supreme Court Throws Lifeline for Tata, Adani, Essar Power Plants,' *LiveMint*, 30 October 2018. Available at https://www.livemint.com/Companies/4H6pXd HODnFBlBrWKaDojO/SC-asks-CERC-to-decide-changes-in-PPAs-for-Tata-Adani-Essa. html (accessed on 24 April 2019).

[21] *Business Standard*, 'States That Procure Power from Tata, Adani's Mundra Miss SC Tariff Deadline,' 2 January 2019. Available at https://www.business-standard.com/article/companies/states-that-procure-power-from-tata-adani-s-mundra-miss-sc-tariff-deadline-119010201127_1.html (accessed on 24 April 2019).

however, resource crunch often limits their ability to do so. Private sector, all over the world, barring a very few countries, has joined hands with the government to create the telecommunication infrastructure and provide services to consumers.

This has led to fierce competition, as one of the primary reasons is the need to keep on upgrading the technology massively frequently. The rate at which telecommunication technology becomes obsolete is miles ahead of the rate of obsolescence in most of the infrastructure sectors such as power, roads, rail and air. Private initiative in leapfrogging in technology requires timely changes to be made in policy by the government. Joint private and public participation is the key to empower people through telecommunication.

Telecom Regulatory Authority of India Act, 1997

The Telecom Regulatory Authority of India (TRAI) was established in 1997 by the Telecom Regulatory Authority of India Act, 1997. It was after the economic liberalization in 1991, the telecommunications sector, along with other sectors, was also opened up gradually from the tight control of government. Private participation was encouraged, though selectively and cautiously. The world had already moved on to the modern telecommunications and India was lagging far behind in the race. Several telecom policies, since then, have progressively increased private participation in providing telecommunications services to the people of India. These services include telephony, internet, Direct-to-Home (DTH) television, etc. Telephony includes the landline services and mobile services.

The extremely fast developments in the mobile phone technology, bringing the information, communication and entertainment together have left the successive governments with no choice but to open the sector for private participation as the government in no way can bridge the gap between demand and supply on its own due to very high aspirations of the consumers. With a lot of telecom business being in the hands of private players, there is always the possibility of excessively high tariffs imposed on the consumers, and to eliminate any such likelihood, the TRAI is mandated to play the role of an independent regulator. Its main role is to regulate services and tariffs, and to create a good business environment for the telecom sector so that the telecom companies can bring in the global standards and operate fairly. Also, it adjudicates upon certain issues and disputes within its jurisdiction, which can be appealed in the Telecom Disputes Settlement and Appellate Tribunal (TDSAT).

The TDSAT was constituted in the year 2000 through an ordinance. It was felt that the TRAI was overly engaged with adjudication and resolution of disputes, and the regulatory framework for telecom was not getting enough attention. To lighten the burden of the TRAI, it was necessary to create another body, and this need resulted in the establishment of the TDSAT. Most of the disputes related to licenses, consumers, etc., are within TDSAT's jurisdiction. It also hears appeals challenging TRAI's decisions. The TDSAT's decision can be appealed in the Supreme Court. Post-economic liberalization, there was a spurt of activity in the telecom sector with the private companies participating in manufacturing telecom equipment, which was mainly assembly of foreign equipment in India and later on shifted to indigenous production also, radio paging which opened the doors for mobile phones within a short period of time, besides plain service of providing telephone connectivity, the real profit was expected in value added services of data usage.

Consumers were not, in general, able to afford the services provided initially and it was understood by the telecom companies, policymakers and everyone connected with telecommunications that the success of telecom revolution was heavily dependent on low prices resulting from fierce competition and supporting policies. Many a time, there were serious issues between several players which needed to be interpreted in the right perspective, and hence quite a few of such matters were decided by the TRAI, appealed in the TDSAT and finally resolved in the Supreme Court.

Heavy investment in the sector by domestic and foreign investors, with necessary periodic tweaking of the telecom policy and interpretations done by the TDSAT and the Supreme Court, paved the way for a bright future for the sector. Consumers rejoiced; however, at times, poor quality of connectivity and data transfer, and high tariffs very often left a bad taste in consumers' mouth. By international standards, India was typically offering one of the lowest rates, which might have looked comparable as statistical data, but were still very high in absolute terms, given the low disposable incomes of majority of Indians. Thus, mobile phones were not able to actually penetrate the real India: the small towns and villages across the continental size country. Mobile towers required very heavy investment and with slow changes in telecom policy, it became attractive for private investment.

In the second decade of the 21st century, India witnessed the unleashing of full-fledged telecom wars between private companies to entice and woo the consumers with never-heard-of offers. Very low tariff and unbelievable services were offered by many companies, resulting in the problem of plenty. Consumers never had it so good. But the financial model for sustainability was quite weak, which prompted the companies to cut corners. Gaps between promises made and performance started widening compelling several subscribers and consumer groups to resort to regulatory and legal remedies. Also, the low mobile tariffs, which were surely not sustainable, left most of the telecom companies in the red which caused a dramatic increase in disputes landing at the TRAI and thereafter at the TDSAT.

Besides fixed and mobile telephones, the number of users of internet in India has gone up dramatically in the last five years or so, especially after the ease of availability and affordability of smartphones along with drastic reduction in price charged for data usage. Entry of a new player Jio in the telecom market changed the equilibrium of business with heavy price reduction. Existing players such as Airtel, Vodafone, Idea, BSNL, Aircel and others cried foul and complained to the TRAI many a time alleging violation of set norms and regulations governing the telecom sector. The regulatory framework has so far been effective in handling complaints and providing remedy at that stage, leading to appeals in the TDSAT and the Supreme Court, beside several political platforms and bureaucratic forums.

Highest levels of competition between service providers do result in benefits for the consumers, and eventually consolidation of companies takes place resulting in fewer players aiming to indeed stay in the market and retain their share, if not increase it. Internet penetration has been positively impacted with the popularly available large screen smartphones, making the landline or broadband connectivity of relevance primarily for commercial use. Monitoring and regulation of the internet for technical reasons such as speed, data usage and format, is to be done for making the performance better and in sync with global changes; however, scrutiny of content sometimes becomes necessary to keep fake news and rumour mongering in check. Convergence of telephone, the internet and entertainment, all through the internet has made the internet the target of many businesses as well as policymakers. The desire to control the internet has made the role of regulators and law enforcers challenging.

The DTH television has developed very fast in India, which earlier was mainly catered by terrestrial television signals and thereafter by cable TV networks. TV was controlled by the government broadcasting service, Doordarshan, which was terrestrial in nature; however, after the liberalization of 1991, cable TV got introduced in the country when many local service providers got the opportunity to start business and make big chunks of money. These service providers were hardly regulated or monitored and there were serious issues of quality of signal as well as the quality of locally produced programmes which were telecast along with the programmes of established and recognized channels.

With the advent of DTH, dish antennae started appearing all over the country with the need to have proper regulation of the technological issues of frequency, bandwidth and related concerns. The TRAI is the institution which regulates DTH also and has to balance the interests of viewers and service providers. One of the important issues is that of tariff fixation. A serious problem in DTH is the bundling of channels by different studios and service providers. With more and more channels catering to different segments of viewers, it is not at all necessary that any particular viewer would like to pay for all the channels, when he watches only a few of them. The approach of 'pay for what you watch' is in consumers' interest and the TRAI has been working on this idea for a long time. Technological advancements have eventually made it really possible to pay only for those channels which an individual or a family watches.

The TRAI has made it compulsory for all broadcasters such as Star and Sony, to classify their programmes in a particular genre to make it easy for the viewer to select among similar offerings. These guidelines have been implemented in early 2019 with tangible benefits for the consumers. However, as most of the broadcasters offer a set of channels as a bouquet, it still has the possibility of viewers subscribing to the entire bouquet rather than unbundling it and selecting a few among them. Moreover, there is somewhere at the back of the mind of a normal and reasonable viewer that it is better, economical and surely easier to subscribe to the entire package rather than a few channels as someday, one may need to view any channel from the bundled set.

That way, the move by the TRAI to bring transparency in tariff fixation by channel selection has caused a lot of confusion in the minds of the people, both viewers and service providers. None of the service providers has remained isolated and immune from TRAI's decisions. But the question is whether the consumers have benefitted or not? Theoretically speaking, yes, as it provides freedom to choose channels of one's choice, but strong criticism by a large body of consumers about the complexity of the procedure to select channels and insufficient information by different channels about the way one should move forward does not make the case for subscribers very strong. It shall be a matter of time when the dust will settle down and true picture emerges.

In 2016, the TRAI ordered the telecom companies to pay to subscribers for call drops, which was challenged by the telecom companies.

CASE STUDY

Cellular Operators Association of India v. TRAI, Supreme Court of India, 2016[22]

In late 2015, the TRAI made certain regulations applicable from January 2016 to make the telecom operators accountable for call drops. For each call drop, the concerned telecom company was supposed to pay ₹1 to the calling subscriber with a maximum of three call drops in a day. It meant that a maximum of ₹90 would have to be paid by the telecom company to the calling subscriber every month, assuming calls dropped very frequently. Considering the revenue model of telecom operators, this would have been a tremendous blow and would have required a huge investment in technological capacity so that calls did not drop, which is quite difficult if not impossible to be achieved, or take this sum into account.

It was a difficult proposition and almost all the telecom operators joined hands to fight the common enemy, TRAI. While getting a licence to do business as the telecom operator in the country, each such company is legally bound to follow the conditions of the licence agreement and also the stipulations made by the telecom regulator TRAI. The purpose of grant of any such licence is to make the private operators serve the consumers in an effective manner with least complaints, and in case any complaints are made, they should be attended and responded at the earliest. Provisions for imposing liquidated damages are also a part of the licence agreement; however, the primary aim is to serve the consumers by providing proper coverage in densely populated districts and towns, and try to spread the coverage and business in scarcely populated rural areas.

---

[22] *Cellular Operators Association of India and others v. Telecom Regulatory Authority of India and others,* Supreme Court of India, 11 May 2016; Bench: R. F. Nariman, Kurian Joseph, JJ.; Reported in: 2016 Indlaw SC 425; (2016) 7 SCC 703; AIR 2016 SC 2336; JT 2016 (5) SC 127; 2016 (4) MLJ 575; 2016(5) SCALE 137; [2016] 9 S.C.R. 1; Civil Appeal No. 5017 of 2016 (Arising Out of S. L. P. (Civil) No. 6521 of 2016) With Civil Appeal No. 5018 of 2016 (Arising Out of S. L. P. (Civil) No. 6522 of 2016).

For a variety of reasons, chiefly because of lack of sufficient number of mobile towers providing proper connectivity, the quality of mobile phone calls had not been satisfactory and many a time while making a conversation, the call would abruptly end without either of the parties hanging up. This experience had been most frustrating for subscribers, and when the subscribers tried to reconnect, as they had to complete the conversation which might at times be only to say bye or thanks, they had to pay again for the new call made, thus, both inconvenience and excess charging, which was something like rubbing salt into the wounds. It was surely double whammy for the subscribers, and numerous complaints with the regulator and the government did not result in an acceptable solution. Being guided by the dictum, spare the rod and spoil the child, the TRAI used the stick, rather than a carrot, and imposed penalty for call drops, which expectedly had the desired impact on the private operators—they immediately took note of it. 'Call drop' was defined as follows:

> 'Call drop' means a voice call which, after being successfully established, is interrupted prior to its normal completion; the cause of early termination is within the network of the service provider....[23]

It was TRAI's view that call drop was a deficiency in service, even according to consumer law, and hence it was the duty of service providers to compensate the consumers for the inconvenience caused.

Service providers, however, were of the opinion that call drop was due to technical reasons and other reasons which were beyond their control, particularly related to spectrum bandwidth, and municipal rules and regulations which were hampering installation of mobile towers at the required places. The regulations were challenged in the Delhi High Court mainly on two grounds: first, the regulations were beyond the powers given by the parent act, and, second, the regulations were arbitrary and unreasonable. The Delhi High Court did

---

[23] Regulation 2 (bb) of the Telecom Consumers Protection Regulations, 2012.

not agree with these grounds and decided in favour of the TRAI by upholding the regulations. The court also held that the compensation of ₹1 for every call drop, with a cap of three call drops a day, was not a penalty but simply notional compensation.

The court observed that it had tried to strike a balance between the interests of subscribers and service providers by upholding the regulations. The high court did not consider the question of difficulty in installation of mobile towers as it observed that such an issue was beyond its purview in that petition. While deciding the matter, the Supreme Court analysed and discussed the arguments made by both the parties and also the consumer groups, which were in favour of upholding TRAI's regulations, and went to the fundamental law which created the TRAI, that is, the TRAI Act, 1997. It was all in the backdrop of the National Telecom Policy, 1994, the telecom services were opened for private participation to provide telecom services of global standards to Indians at reasonable and affordable price along with creating conducive environment for business in the telecom sector.

The TRAI Act, 1997, provided for the establishment of the authority—TRAI—for regulating the telecommunication services in the country and matters related to it. The adjudicatory function of the authority was taken away in 2000 and vested in the TDSAT. Deciding the question of whether the regulation was within the provisions of the TRAI Act or not, the Supreme Court held that because the licence conditions for the telecom operators already provided for 2 per cent of call drop every month as permissible, and the role of the regulatory body TRAI was not only to see the interest of consumers but to find the proper balance between the consumers' interests and the interests of the telecom operators, the regulation was against the basic purpose of the parent act and, hence, was beyond the powers of delegated legislation and could not be legally tenable.

Thus, it was ultra vires the parent act. On the question of arbitrariness, the Supreme Court observed that consumer interest cannot be the justification of any arbitrary action. Hence, even if the challenged regulation was in the interest of consumers, it must pass the test of not being arbitrary independently. After discussing a number of decided cases and applying the principles laid down in those cases, the Supreme Court was of the clear view that the regulation was indeed arbitrary and not based on any logical thinking. It was admitted by the TRAI that the reasons for call drop were not only attributable to the service provider but also to the subscriber, and data had shown that more than one-third of the call drops happen due to the subscribers' fault.

Thus, it would have been obviously unfair to penalize the service provide even for the fault of subscribers. The Supreme Court, therefore, held that the regulation was unfair, unreasonable and arbitrary. Interestingly, the amendment in the year 2000, which took away the adjudicatory functions from the TRAI, had left the TRAI only with the administrative and legislative functions, and the adjudication of disputes was to be done by the TDSAT. This is very different from the other sectors, for instance, electricity, where the law, the Electricity Act, 2003, vests the CERC and different SERCs with quasi-judicial powers also besides the administrative and legislative powers. The decision of the legislature in making the amendment in the telecom sector regulatory law to have separate institutions for regulatory functions and adjudicatory functions has been well thought and based on data and research.

The TRAI was expected to focus and channelize all its resources—time, effort, expertise, etc.—on regulation so that the policies formulated and regulations made could be in tune with the best in the world and at the same time be within the constitutional and legal framework of India. Regarding the question of modifying the licence between the service provider and a subscriber, which is a contract between two willing parties, the Supreme Court held that the terms of the contract cannot be modified by the regulatory body, until and unless mandated by the governing law and the legislative body. In this case, the TRAI's regulation did not fit in this exception, and hence it could not impose the challenge regulation on the parties to a contract, without the consent of both the parties.

Obviously, the subscribers wished to get that benefit, but the private operator would not agree for commercial and strategic reasons. It is also the duty of the TRAI, and all regulators, to act with transparency, which means openness in governance and taking into consideration the views of all the stakeholders and thereafter make decisions based on these views in a logical manner. The challenged regulation was made after due consultation with all the stakeholders, but views of service providers were not duly considered as is obvious from the fact that the regulation was one-sided and benefitted the subscribers only.

Though legislative functioning is not necessarily supposed to take into account the views of the affected parties, it may not be applicable to the regulatory bodies performing legislative functions as is true for legislative bodies with plenary powers. The telecom companies were able to win the legal battle; however, to remain competitive in the market in a sustainable manner it is important for them to be able to win over the subscribers, which can only be done when value for money is ensured and technologically the services are upgraded periodically to match the best in the world. Heavy investment is essential for providing the telecom services seamlessly and ROI can be painful and excruciatingly slow. It is a game of patience, perseverance and endurance.

Court battles do not typically help the telecom companies in getting more business, though they may be good for proving a point as far as regulators are concerned. Even with the regulators, it is not at all advisable for the telecom companies to rub them the wrong way. Willy-nilly the telecom companies have to play the game according to the rules set by the regulators, which can be damaging in the long run, if there is constant tussle between them. The TRAI, as a regulator, is no exception and telecom companies, broadly speaking, have understood to live in peace with it.

KEY TAKEAWAYS

- *Sectoral regulators:* There are regulatory bodies for different sectors of infrastructure, and investors and businesses working in specific sectors should focus on the manner in which these regulators work. Keeping a track of orders and decisions made by them helps the business executives in making well-informed decisions. The sector-specific regulators are in addition to the sectoral regulators, which have their reach on almost all the businesses.

- *Early stage:* Business executives have to appreciate the fact that most of the sector-specific regulators in India have been newly created in the last two decades or so and, hence, these are in the early stage of evolution. It will take time for the regulators to progress to the level of expertise and professionalism as experienced in the developed countries. Thus, businesses need to be patient and not condemn each and every decision of these regulators.

- *Judicial friction:* To smoothen the rough edges of sector-specific regulators, many matters are appealed in appellate tribunals and courts. This is a continuous exercise and in the early stages of the development of regulatory bodies, decisions of courts, especially the Supreme Court of India, are significant in firming the contours of the regulations and the interplay of law and regulations.

Chapter 3
LAWS AND REGULATIONS ACROSS SECTORS

Infrastructure projects are characterized by high sunk cost. In PPP projects, this cost has to be borne by the private party and, therefore, it is a big risk to be taken by the private business. As is quite obvious, any private business would like to make a substantial profit at the end of the day and, hence, investing money in a PPP should eventually be a profitable venture for the private business, which can only be ensured with proper government participation and backing. In democratic countries, governments are answerable to the people. It makes it quite natural for the governments to try to appease the common man. Thus, it is not in the interest of the governments to increase the tariffs. But, on the other hand, it is necessary for the businesses to have higher tariff fixation, so as to be able to make profits.

Regulatory bodies have to play the important role of balancing the interest of consumers and businesses at the same time. This is a tightrope walk. Very often, regulatory bodies are not able to do so, because of being pulled in different directions by various players in the field. Lower tariffs can be achieved by encouraging competition among players willing to take up PPP projects. This competition, ideally, should be fair. It is rather difficult to ensure fairness in all situations as we all live in a real world—as contradistinguished with an ideal world—with everyone working, like the rational economic man, to maximize one's own interest, often pecuniary in nature.

In the real world, the rational economic man usually works in conflicting situations where other persons are also working to maximize their own self-interest, and this endeavour leads many of them to cut each other's paths which is truly not beneficial for the society. This is surely not the purpose of a civilized society, which aims to provide circumstances for each and every person to rise to his or her own full potential. Without any control and supervision, unregulated markets experience forces in different directions, often looking to achieve short-term goals rather than long-term and strategic targets. This is not a desirable situation which results in wasteful dissipation of societal energy without any positive movement in the direction of the set target. This phenomenon necessitates regulation of the current tasks being done and also proper planning and execution of the future works.

MARKET FAILURES AND REGULATION

It has been experienced that without any regulation and control, simple market forces—demand and supply—do not create a proper and well-determined set-up for the businesses. Market forces simply left to work on their own usually do not result in high efficiency from the point of view of the society at large. Thus, the society finally is at a loss, as goods and services required by a highly efficient society do not result in being produced, or consumed, in the expected manner. Therefore, it means that the market fails in achieving the highest social value. This is not at all the optimal solution and requires intervention by the government or independent regulators to ensure corrective action.

The regulatory intervention by the government is typically in situations where the market fails to provide effective means to achieve the set objectives of the government. In dictatorships, the role of government intervention is, for all practical purposes, absolute and because of this reason the businesses get used to being dictated by the government as to what to do and what not to do. But, in case of democratic societies with elected governments, the situation is a bit different as the people have the freedom to choose a lot many things, including the government of the day and, hence, it is not obvious for them to be directed by the government for their business actions. The role of the government in regulating different businesses in true democratic countries is ticklish and is often guided by exigencies; however, for long-term and sustainable businesses, it is important that the government's role as a regulator is unbiased, bipartisan and, to the extent possible, apolitical.

At times, the government tries to regulate certain sectors by using contractual clauses, especially in PPP, but the real test of these contracts is the effectiveness of the legal environment in which the contracts have to be enforced. Legal validity of contracts is questionable when the sovereign powers, according to their own convenience and self-interest, choose to honour the contract or treat it like a piece of waste paper. A contractual arrangement may give a sense of freedom to the private business entity but practically it may only be an indirect control by the public entity using legal provisions and the judicial set-up.

Market failures necessitate regulation; however, political issues truly remain in a commanding position for regulatory action. Whenever there is something missing in the economy, politics takes over and provides a new regulatory framework to solve the problem. It is not at all necessary that the political solution is really based on sound economic reasoning. Many a time, these solutions, guided by the exigencies of politics, remain relevant for a particular period of time and, thereafter, maybe simply pushed towards irrelevance. Regulatory measures provide tremendous opportunities for businesses to exploit the system at a particular period of time and thereafter make suitable moves to create opportunities for commercial exploitation in the future. The role of bureaucrats is crucial in making it possible for the businesses to make open commercially viable options.

INFRASTRUCTURE AS PUBLIC GOODS

Infrastructure as public goods has to serve everyone and it is not possible to exclude some persons from using it. Two important features of public goods—non-excludability and non-rivalry, which are also true for intellectual property rights to a large extent—make it difficult to control them with market forces. Non-excludability means that it is not possible to exclude a certain section of people from using the public goods, and non-rivalry in consumption means that if there are more number of people using certain public goods, the value received by others is small in number and does not get reduced. Thus, neither the cost of providing that public good goes up if the number of people enjoying it increases, nor the benefit to them lessens with more people joining in. These two features of public goods apply directly to infrastructure creation whether it is roads, sanitation, cleanliness, education, etc.

There is, however, a fact which cannot be neglected that the increase in the number of people consuming certain public goods will surely create problems of maintaining a proper sequence of persons who can enjoy the benefits, and thereby assuring that there is no chaos and unruly behaviour by the large number of people who would like to take advantage of the available public goods. This itself leads to some sort of control or regulation. The increase in the number of people does not always necessary mean increase in revenue flow as a good number of people would be interested to enjoy the benefits of the public goods for free which leads to free riding as they cannot be stopped only by market forces.

Benefits of infrastructure creation cannot always directly be reserved for the people who pay for it simply because of the two characteristics discussed earlier: non-excludability and non-rivalry. A free riding persists, no one is willing to pay as it is easy to anticipate that one can always free ride and enjoy the benefits so why should one pay. And, if no one is willing to pay, the infrastructure as public goods can never be created in the first place. Thus, it is a peculiar problem that without making someone to pay for creation of infrastructure, it will never be created, and if no infrastructure is created there is certainly no growth and development.

Hence, free riding has to be minimized, if not eliminated, as far as infrastructure creation and usage are concerned. It becomes a serious issue in egalitarian societies with socialistic leanings. When wealth creation becomes almost akin to committing sin, private enterprise takes a back seat and very easily washes its hands off any such responsibility which may bring a bad name to it and possibly label it as a practitioner of crony capitalism. However, free riding has to be minimized to ensure optimal use of available resources so that undeserving and non-paying people do not take the public goods created for granted. It brings us to the issue of externalities in the creation, maintenance and usage of infrastructure.

Externalities, as the name suggests, are those forces which have an impact on the overall quality of life of an individual due to the actions of some other person. There may not be a direct targeted action by individual towards another individual; however, there is an indirect impact which may not at all be possible to easily quantify and measure tangibly.

For instance, keeping the surroundings clean is positive for everyone who uses those surroundings and, thus, is clearly a positive externality; however, keeping them filthy is undoubtedly a negative externality which is in one way or the other harmful for everyone. If everyone thinks that by keeping the surroundings clean, he or she is creating a positive environment but is not being paid for by anyone, there is no direct benefit to maintain cleanliness and thus will not do it.

Therefore, the positive externality in the absence of any incentive for the good doer may turn into a negative externality as the same person does not keep the place clean, rather has no qualms in littering it. The only solution to such a problem is to penalize the negative conduct and incentivize positive behaviour. It can be done either economically or through other means of social recognition. Making people pay for everything that they consume is one way of solving the problem of negative externality; however, everything cannot be unbundled and day-to-day life will come to a standstill if one is expected to pay for every ray of sunlight received and every molecule of oxygen inhaled.

LEGAL FRAMEWORK FOR INFRASTRUCTURE

The basic legal system followed in a particular jurisdiction determines how the infrastructure laws shall be structured. The British system of 'common law', which is primarily based on binding precedents, is the legal system followed in almost all the Commonwealth countries, including India. However, most of the European countries follow the system of 'civil law' which is based on a civil code rather than binding precedents. The civil law countries are distinguished by the dominance of administrative law, which has grown by leaps and bounds in the last century due to new frontiers of administration and governance, with infrastructure being one of the major sectors of growth and development. It is often difficult to have contractual arrangements deviating from set administrative principles.

Sovereign countries, following either the civil law or the common law system, do have the inherent power to have a legal framework of their choice; however, they do follow some of the well-established norms of commercial transactions, contracts, legal remedies, etc. There are lesser or almost no restrictions on contracts for infrastructure in common law countries as compared to civil law countries, with the condition that the contractual terms must be within the legal framework. Anything beyond that framework does not remain enforceable. The PPP projects are restrained by the voluntarily agreed terms between the parties; however, 'public interest' can be the guiding factor in determining the enforceable meaning of the clauses. This, in a sense, is curtailing the freedom of the parties to a contract by bringing in newer facets of administrative law into consideration.

Limiting the scope of the almost infinite canvas of PPP agreements, the purist approach to contracts—treating them impregnable by any external factor other than the parties to the contract—does not work in practical situations. Though it is not necessary to have specific laws enacted for PPPs for infrastructure development, some jurisdictions prefer to do it. These specific PPP laws may be enacted for different sectors, or for PPPs across sectors. There is no hard and fast rule about it. The laws such enacted for PPPs and other laws must necessarily be in consonance so as to avoid any friction between the two. Obviously, the PPP-specific laws shall be within the larger framework of the general legal system and, hence, these can never be in conflict with the generally applicable system.

Infusion of adequate finance and the laws for hedging the risks taken by investors depend on the broad legal system, which is narrowed down to specific rules and regulations to take care of the smallest of the issues. These may wary from, for instance, the case of insolvency to target winding up of the defaulter or encouraging him somehow to bring the business back on the track and pay back. The legal systems ensure proper governance and accountability. Effectiveness of financial documents and administrative decisions requires transparency, and it depends heavily on the legal system governing administration. Civil law jurisdictions usually tend to be less transparent as compared to common law countries.

The legal framework for infrastructure and PPPs also includes policies made by the governments—central and state—from time to time. The legal environment for infrastructure creation gets the proper perspective from the policy documents, which are modified according to the needs and aspirations. The role of public sector companies along with the private companies is to be fixed according to the constitutional provisions and other statutes governing the infrastructure. The public sector companies have to comply with strict provisions, which for private companies are not that stringent. Levels of transparency and accountability are very high in public sector companies, which are open to public glare and thus scrutiny. Finance availability is usually a function of the ease of recovering money, rate of interest, risks involved and the duties to be performed by different parties to a contract.

The public sector is also bound by the stringent constitutional requirements of following the provisions of fundamental rights, like the right to equality and non-discrimination. The complex PPPs are of value only and only if the legal environment supports them with fair treatment, proper regulatory controls and efficacious resolution of disputes. The legal environment should aim at reducing the transaction costs and thereby improving the overall efficiency of the system. The Indian legal system, especially whatever is relevant for infrastructure development, is changing slowly to align itself with the latest legal norms practised in the other jurisdictions of the world. The long-standing demands of foreign investors are to make the procedural law and practice in India less cumbersome and more effective. Efforts are being made in this direction.

INFRASTRUCTURE REGULATION: INSTRUMENTS AND INSTITUTIONS

The regulatory institutions are the creation of legal instruments, the laws enacted by the competent legislative body. Regulation, interestingly, combines legislation and litigation both. The regulatory institutions write their own rules within the framework of the respective laws which have created them and execute these rules with certain executive powers. Most of the regulatory institutions also perform the role of adjudication with expert opinion being made available by subject matter experts as members of the tribunal. Usually, domain experts complement legal experts making the adjudicatory tribunal body having expertise both in law and the subject matter in question. The regulatory institutions also perform the role of prosecutors, and thus it can very well be concluded that the regulatory institutions have immense power, though it has to be exercised within the legal framework.

There are, many a time, members of regulatory institutions with background and experience of being a bureaucrat in the government. In business, competitors do lobby with these bureaucrats, while they are in office, to get policies tweaked to their advantage and get certain policies enforced against competitors. These bureaucrats, while working as members in regulatory institutions, have to perform a very different role—that of an independent and impartial regulator and not as someone who is part and parcel of the government. Making this transition is often difficult from the perspective of seeing things in an independent fashion and from a specialist's point of view. Infrastructure is one sector which has been one of the most lucrative area for bureaucrats in their career.

India has been on the path of development and creation of infrastructure since independence; however, there have been ups and downs in this process. Most of the bureaucrats have experienced these changes themselves or have got to know about them with the help of their colleagues, who serve as unfathomable treasure of knowledge, experience and, most importantly, anecdotes. This is all extremely valuable while working in any regulatory institution; however, there is a hang-over and heavy baggage also associated with them. Past experiences and opinions formed by getting to know about certain companies and business leaders from others—this knowledge can be from rumours, hearsay, pure fiction or, as is called nowadays, fake news, etc.—have the possibility of biased decision-making defeating to a certain extent, if not completely, the very purpose of the creation of an independent regulator.

Infrastructure development in the fast lane, the number of regulations has gone up enormously and, at times, it is very difficult for any company to comply with each one of them. To do business by being on the right side of the law, it is essential to comply fully and for this very purpose people with deep knowledge of the regulatory framework and with the ability to anticipate changes to be made are appointed at senior positions in different companies. Their job is not only to make their company comply but also to be on the look out for any lapse on the part of their competitors so as to catch them immediately on the wrong foot.

The importance of regulatory institutions in infrastructure is arguably strategic, as the competitors use regulations to fight the business battle, which otherwise would have been fought in the market, and in evolved jurisdictions, possibly in courts of law. The existence of regulatory bodies provides a fantastic option for the competitors to play the regulatory chess by remaining in the background, which is quite possible as the regulatory instruments and institutions encourage any person to bring to the notice of the regulator any amiss and remiss. Thereafter, it is the job of the regulator to investigate and take proper action. This is a fantastic arrangement for businesses which can get the benefit of getting their competitors in hot water without doing anything substantial. This tendency makes the job of a regulator highly responsible and it is expected that they would entertain any complaint only after proper initial scrutiny. Regulators also set the standards especially for technologically oriented businesses.

GUJARAT INFRASTRUCTURE DEVELOPMENT BOARD

The state of Gujarat has been at the forefront of industrial development for almost half a century with the enactment of the Gujarat Industrial Development Act of 1962, which led to the establishment of Gujarat Industrial Development Corporation (GIDC) for expediting the industrialization of the state. Establishment of different industries in faraway locations in the state created industrial estates which required a proper connectivity by roads, power supply, water, telecommunication and everything needed for day-to-day living. With the passage of time, different industrial estates emerged as small townships with growth of population in nearby areas. As we have discussed that the pace of economic development and industrialization slowed down for about three decades and it was only after economic liberalization in 1991 that a new ray of hope was visible.

Changes in policies definitely had their positive impact and the eagerness and the willingness of the private sector to invest was visible to the political leadership. By the turn of the last century, it was the right time to enact a new law for the holistic development of infrastructure in the state of Gujarat. There was an urgent need to put everything together, especially at the policy formulation level, with clarity of thought and clarity of purpose so as to achieve the goal of infrastructure development with the least possible impediments and within the shortest period of time. To convince the investors, it was the need of the hour to have the blueprint ready so that they could anticipate future growth and development, and could also gauge the ROI.

With this background, the Gujarat Infrastructure Development Act (GIDA), 1999, was enacted and came into force in April 1999. The Act provided for the establishment of Gujarat Infrastructure Development Board (GIDB), which had already been established in 1995, but was given the statutory status after the enactment of the GIDA, 1999. The primary purpose of establishment of the GIDB was to have sustainable growth and development of the infrastructure sector along with a balanced approach followed towards the social sector. Only industrial growth, without taking the society along, would not have given the desired results in the long run. After all, industries exist for society and not the other way round. The GIDB works with a large framework of experts, who are from different domains essential for infrastructure.

They come with legal, technical, commercial, financial, administrative, managerial, social and behavioural, environmental, etc., expertise. The GIDA gave the legal framework for working with the PPP model, which was fundamentally based on a win-win situation both for public and private sector. Any business entity would never want to lose money in the long run and will not like to be emotionally blackmailed using patriotic or inequality platforms to serve the nation. Social services and doing something for the country sound good to a businessman for a short period of time; however, if one wants to have his money, time and attention, one has to show him profits at the end of the day. And that's precisely what the GIDA and the GIDB were able to do.

New methods in PPP—some of them had already been tested in the Western world—were used on experimental basis in pilot projects. Competitive bidding was the mantra for getting good quality work done at the lowest cost and inviting willing and expert private parties to contribute to infrastructure development and at the same time make decent money for themselves. The GIDA also made provisions for comparative bidding and direct negotiations in certain cases. The Swiss challenge method, which involves giving a chance to private parties to make unsolicited offers and if approved by the government or the public authority to match the lowest bid was also tried to take the advantage of innovative ideas. The GIDB works towards a single window clearance system, as private parties had perennially complained about going from one desk to another to get their file cleared and not even being sure of the place where one should apply for something.

The GIDB is the nodal agency for the Delhi–Mumbai Industrial Corridor Project (DMIC), which is the dedicated 1,500 km industrial corridor connecting Delhi and Mumbai.

It is a huge infrastructure project in which Japan has invested substantially. The GIDB is the apex authority under the Gujarat Special Investment Region (SIR) Act, 2009, which empowers the state government to establish SIRs, so as not to get into the quagmire of routine legal and administrative difficulties. The GIDB performs advisory, coordinating and regulatory functions and has been a success story so far, as has been seen in 2014 by foreign observers,[24] with the greatest success being witnessed in the ports sector, which it wishes to replicate in other infrastructure sectors.

KELKAR COMMITTEE REPORT ON PPP

The GoI had set up a committee to evaluate the PPP model of infrastructure development in early 2015 as the PPP model had slowed down a lot after the initial euphoria, experienced at the turn of the century, which continued for less than a decade. There were serious problems of blocked resources in pending PPP projects, and infrastructure sector was going through a lean phase. To infuse new energy in the infrastructure sector, it was necessary to give stimulus to PPP, as the government on its own could not muster enough resources to take the projects forward and surely not to the final stage of completion.

Vijay Kelkar, noted economist, was heading the committee, and that's why the committee was called the 'Kelkar Committee on Revisiting and Revitalising the PPP Model of Infrastructure Development' and its terms of reference mainly mentioned reviewing the experience of PPP policy in India and suggesting

---

[24] *Firstpost*, 'Gujarat Has a Strong System to Enable PPP Projects: Report,' 20 December 2014. Available at https://www.firstpost.com/business/economy/gujarat-has-a-strong-system-to-enable-ppp-projects-report-459754.html (accessed on 24 April 2019).

measures to improve capacity building for effective implementation. In a sense, the committee had been given a very broad scope and almost anything plaguing the PPPs in India could have been covered. The committee submitted its report in less than a year, by the end of 2015. Mainly, the report suggested securing easy funding for PPP projects. It appeared to be the most obvious observation as PPP projects are disputed, suspended or abandoned mostly because of lack of funds, and the other most important reason being denial of environmental, land acquisition or other approvals by competent authorities.

The committee recommended that for securing adequate funds, it was necessary to disclose the long-term costs, risks and other issues to the private parties willing to enter into CAs. Negotiation and re-negotiation of these agreements should ideally be after making the parties fully aware of the complete known facts and anticipated risks and rewards. Good faith and trust in the dealing between the government and the private parties were the essential conditions for any successful negotiation exercise leading to satisfactorily completed projects. The committee had laid great emphasis on transparency and disclosure. The committee recommended independent sector-specific regulators for resolving pending issues; however, it has been observed that big ticket projects are never finally resolved at the regulator level; most of them are appealed in the appellate authorities and thereafter in the Supreme Court.

The recommendation of the committee seems to be more of a general observation rather than a practical and realistic idea. Another recommendation was to modify the PPP model according to the experience by the government for about a decade. This was to say that the parties should move higher on the learning curve and make the agreements more detailed and refined. However, this does not work particularly in highly litigious jurisdictions like India, for the simple reason of availability of too many appeals and easy accessibility to the courts. Among other things, the committee also recommended strongly the creation of an infrastructure centre of excellence, 3P India, a think tank for providing expertise in preparing better contracting models and dispute redressal systems.

The committee recommended that the government should encourage banks and financial institutions to give loans for PPP projects at discounted rates, which somehow does not make sense as managing the functioning of banks and other financial institutions is to be done on commercial basis and with keeping the risk in mind. To avoid any bad debts and non-performing assets (NPAs), they are supposed to work on pure commercial basis without the interference of the government. If they start following the advice of the government, their autonomy is gone and they cannot function in a business-like manner. The committee came heavily on the Swiss challenge method, which is based on unsolicited proposals, as they result in opacity and unequal treatment of parties.

Moreover, the basic idea of getting the best party to do the job gets defeated and, many a time with this method followed, there have been incidents of improper procurement and favouritism. At the same time of this report, the Indian Railways has gone ahead with this method at a large number of railway stations for their modernization. The committee strongly recommended that any of the state-owned PSUs should not be allowed to bid for PPP projects and that PPPs should not be adopted for very small projects, as it has been experienced that PPP is neither effective nor economical for very small and small projects. The government should not bind itself for projects which have low stakes. Finally, the report was all for fully exploiting commercially the risk taking ability of the private sector.

PUBLIC PROCUREMENT

Governments all over the world purchase goods and services, and this is done through different ministries, departments, public sector undertakings (PSUs), municipal bodies, etc. In India, public procurement is done by the government and other public bodies to get the best value of the money spent by using the principle of competition among sellers of goods and service providers as most of them aspire to be supplying goods or services to the government. Usually, government orders are humongous and there is a certain degree of prestige associated with being a government supplier in the society. So there is no dearth of suppliers and vendors who compete to give the best offer to the government. Centralized procurement with standard specifications makes the competition tougher as the overall profit with a large number of units supplied becomes substantial. This helps in getting the goods and services at a fair price. Public procurement, according to Indian legal system, has to be transparent and must give equal opportunity to everyone, rather than picking up someone arbitrarily. As the information about the goods and services to be procured is in public domain—and it has to be well disseminated—there are possibilities of unscrupulous suppliers in colluding and price fixing. Methods such as auction, e-auction and two-stage bidding, are used to minimize—ideal situation will be to eliminate—the chance of unfair practices being followed. The power of choosing a particular offer with a private sector organization is almost absolute; however, government does not have that luxury and must exercise discretion with caution and taking into account all the legal and regulatory requirements.

Government eMarketplace

There are extensive checks and balances to ensure that the discretionary power is exercised properly without favouring anyone or intentionally hurting any party. Centralized procurement done by the government through Directorate General of Supplies and Disposals (DGS&D) for more than 100 years—it started during the British time—was given a modern look in 2017 by shutting down DGS&D and starting Government eMarketplace (GeM). A dedicated e-market was created for procuring goods and services for the government organizations and public sector. It is an online platform, which provides an opportunity to almost anyone willing to sell goods or services from anywhere in the country. Geographical barriers have been demolished by this platform. Also, there is complete transparency and as the entire process is online, it is speedy and efficient with complete transactions recorded digitally. Different tools are available on the online platform for e-bidding, reverse e-auction, etc. It has been legalized through an entry in 2017 in the Government of India (Allocation of Business) Rules, 1961, to the effect 'Development, operation and maintenance of National Public Procurement Portal—Government eMarketplace'.[25] GeM has grown rapidly and is being taken seriously. Many state governments have signed Memorandum of Understanding (MoU) with GeM for procuring their goods and services through GeM platform, and a sizeable number of small and medium size suppliers are quite happy with the development.

---

[25] https://gem.gov.in/aboutus (accessed on 24 April 2019).

Prior to the online platform, small vendors were not able to get even the information, forget about mustering courage to participate in the bidding process.

Competition Commission of India

The Competition Commission of India (CCI) has a very important role in regulating public procurement. In cases of corrupt practices such as bid rigging, cartelization, price fixing, creating entry barriers and abusing dominant position, the CCI is empowered to take corrective and punitive action according to the Competition Act, 2002. The primary function of the CCI is to intervene in cases capable of effecting competition in India adversely. The CCI goes deep into the finer aspects to pick up the right signals of anti-competitive behaviour and can work on specific indicators like a very small number of companies entering into bidding every time for the same type of work, and that too repeatedly. Other pointers can be understood by keenly watching the market conditions, including the technology used. There are detailed booklets, brochures, presentations, etc., prepared by the CCI to be disseminated to industry and other concerned professionals as a part of its advocacy programme. The basic premise on which the CCI works is the alignment of business and legal strategy, so that the businesses remain on the right side of the law. Using strategic tools for achieving the higher business goals of higher profits, along with growth and development, is absolutely fine, but the CCI tries to make sure that everything is done within the letter and spirit of law. Building entry barriers for any new entrant by dominant players is a very old strategy and cannot be controlled by market forces if left unregulated. The same applies to use of substitutes, which may emerge due to technological changes and development, and can be simply shunned by government decisions. The CCI, as an independent and professional institution, has the role of providing a level playing field to all the players in the market and keep the doors open for innovative ideas.

KEY TAKEAWAYS

- *Public goods:* The unique problem of infrastructure being public goods is that infrastructure cannot be reserved only for people who pay for it. Issues of free riding are rampant, and economic management is essential to make the infrastructure projects financially viable. Creation of public infrastructure has to be paid by some but later enjoyed by everyone.

- *Infrastructure regulation:* Market forces are not able to result in high efficiency if left to work on their own. Hence, regulation is essential to achieve highest social value. Regulatory bodies perform both legislative and adjudicatory functions.

- *Public procurement:* In democratic countries like India, public procurement is challenging as the best quality has to be procured at the lowest price. Transparency is an essential feature of public procurement, and accountability has to be fixed for proper legal remedies in cases of misuse or abuse of discretionary power.

Chapter 4
CHALLENGES TO INFRASTRUCTURE DEVELOPMENT IN INDIA

There are many challenges to infrastructure development in India. Ironically, the most important are at the basic level of planning and policy formulation, which lead to defects in bid design and CAs. The perception that execution is weak and most of the defects lie at the stage of implementation of plans is not wholly true. Though there is some truth in it, the serious issue is with the planning itself. For instance, use of the most appropriate technology for any infrastructure project is often neglected and the requisite thinking is not done for the main reason that either the right technology is not identified at the point in time or, even if identified, getting access to proprietary technology is often a big concern due to complexities of licensing agreements and typically high licensing fee.

Most of the cutting-edge technology in major infrastructure sectors is owned by foreign companies and despite emphasis on research and development in India, there is still a long way to go when we, in India, will be pushing the technology frontier in the country itself. Heavy dependence on technology transfer in a legally clean manner is one of the biggest challenges. There have been several cases of breach of intellectual property rights in technology transfer to Indian companies being litigated in courts and other forums in India and abroad. Smooth flow of technology with clear guidelines and sharply defined contours of usage will make this challenge surmountable.

The other challenges are the problems associated with lack of depth and clarity in the bid design documents and CAs. The MCAs prepared by the erstwhile Planning Commission and later followed by different ministries of the government, either as they were or with some tweaking, leave much to be desired. The PPPs require conditions to be made which aim at a win-win situation for the public and private partners; every risk cannot be passed to the private party. Somehow, the MCAs do not follow this basic idea, and in the zeal to protect the 'public' aspect, the CAs are so lopsided that the private parties are highly suspicious of each and every word and even punctuation mark used in the document.

Many a time, the RfP and RfQ documents are the cause of litigation. Issues related to cartelization and bid rigging definitely pose a big challenge to the fairness of the entire process of two-stage bidding and allotting the work to the lowest bidder. Price fixing due to collusion still persists in the infrastructure sector despite the competition law and the action taken by the CCI in several matters. One of the reasons is delay and uncertainty in execution of the fines imposed, which itself is quite low by global standards. To bring transparency in the system, getting most of the things done electronically through e-bidding, e-tendering and e-auction is a good step and will, hopefully, cleanse the system fully in the near future.

Two major challenges faced by almost all the infrastructure projects, however, are land acquisition and environmental clearances.

LAND ACQUISITION AND PPPs

For infrastructure projects, land is essential as most of the projects deal with roads, bridges, tunnels, buildings, railway stations, airports, dams, power generating units or T&D lines, telecommunication towers, canals, river banks, seaports, etc. Nothing can be done until and unless sufficient area of land is available for construction of different facilities, and this means that the government or the private party, in a PPP project, must have control over the land. In dictatorships and communist countries where the governments commonly have a strong hold on the people and their property, getting control over any piece of land is not at all difficult and can be done simply by an executive order without the possibility of it being challenged anywhere; however, in democratic countries with strong rule of law and judicial system like India, each and every such order can be challenged in a court of law on the basis of property rights and not adhering to the established administrative procedure. This can be a nightmare for the managers of a PPP project.

Usually the private businesses find it very difficult, or next to impossible, to get control over large tracts of land as simple principles of economics—demand and supply—come into operation as soon as a private entity makes its intention known to the people of a particular area that it wishes to procure large tracts of land. The price of land spirals up, and there may be a few persons who hold out, with extreme patience, for the supply of the land to go down, and then the buyer being compelled to negotiate with them for their piece of land without which there cannot be a continuous stretch of usable land. Private businesses do not have the power of the sovereign to use their authority to acquire any piece of land for public purpose compulsorily. In such a scenario, it is the government which can use its power, within the framework of law, to acquire land compulsorily from the unwilling landowners on the grounds of public interest and public purpose.

We need to remember that democratic governments are elected by the people of the country and, hence, public interest is paramount, and almost anything can be done on the pretext of public welfare, public purpose, public interest, public use, etc. There have often been questions raised about the real purpose of land acquisition by the governments of the day, both in India and in other countries, as many a time it has been experienced that the land acquired by the government has been transferred in the name of private businesses, in one way or another, without any apparent public purpose being served. The compulsory acquisition of land is often known as eminent domain or expropriation. Whatever one may call it, compulsory land requisition is without the willingness of the landowner to part with this land and, therefore, it is the duty of the government to compensate the landowner adequately and promptly.

Often the rate at which the governments acquire land is much below the market price, which may fluctuate rapidly depending on the current development around the land and future projects planned nearby. The governments typically stick to one specific rate for a unit area of land for several years in a particular locality which obviously loses any connection with the real market rate with the passage of time. Whether the landowners like it or not, compulsory acquisition of land is essential for the creation of proper infrastructure and it cannot be done away with in almost all the jurisdictions of the world. Markets on their own are not able to respond to the needs of the society regarding infrastructure projects as far as land acquisition is concerned and often result in delay, or excessive pricing, or both. Many a time, certain infrastructure projects simply remain on paper because of problems faced in land acquisition by the private players. The government necessarily has to intervene in these situations.

The role of the government does not end after acquiring the land compulsorily as it has to take care of the people who have been displaced because of such acquisition. The rehabilitation of the people according to their societal norms and also providing them sufficient means of livelihood at some other place is not always possible—for the simple reason that two places, however similar they may be, cannot be identical—and at the same time to work as a calming balm on the deeply abraded mental state of being uprooted from their original place is a tall order.

LAND ACQUISITION LAW IN INDIA

In India, the law for acquiring land for a long time had been the Land Acquisition Act, 1894, which made the provision for acquiring land for public purpose. This law was repealed and a new law came into effect on 1 January 2014. It is known as the Right to Fair Compensation and Transparency in Land Acquisition, Rehabilitation and Resettlement (RFCTLARR) Act, 2013. It is a law made by federal legislature and has been enacted to take care of serious problems faced by the landowners due to the earlier law of 1894. Primarily, the earlier law did not have any effective provision for the rehabilitation and resettlement (R&R) of the landowners and also the people who were dependent on that particular piece of land for their livelihood and social well-being.

There were not enough provisions for having realistic consultation with the affected parties and there were not adequate efforts made to acquire only an optimum size of land for the public purpose as mentioned in the notification for acquiring land and approved by competent body. Usually, the tendency was to acquire more land than necessary which often led to wastage of land. The compensation as determined under the previous law was very often inadequate and not according to the market value of the land. Sometimes, chunks of land were acquired using the special provision of urgency, bypassing the normal and routinely followed procedure which typically takes care of protection of the legal rights of landowners, including the principles of natural justice which have been duly incorporated in the detailed procedure.

In India, land acquisition is a concurrent subject, which means the federal legislature as well as the state legislatures can make the law on this subject. There should not be, however, any conflict between the two laws, and in case there are provisions which are in conflict, the central law prevails. This is the fundamental principle followed in almost all the cases wherein both the central government and the state governments have the power to make the laws according to the Constitution of India. The Seventh Schedule of the Constitution of India provides three lists: the Union list as list I, the State list as list II and the Concurrent list as list III. Only the central legislature can make laws on subjects listed in list I, the state legislatures can make laws on subjects listed in list II and both the central and state legislatures can make laws on subjects listed in list III.

Thus, according to the Constitution, land has not been made only under the control of the central government but the state governments have enough powers to decide matters related to land. This is truly a balancing act reflecting the federal structure of the Constitution. This is an important provision because the central government may require land, at times, for issues related to national interest—which may be safety and security, or something of great national importance—and sometimes urgently, and the state governments may not cooperate, perhaps due to certain political reasons, and if land is not made available to the central government it may be detrimental to the entire nation.

The land acquisition law in the country is to safeguard the interests of landowners and others dependent on a particular piece of land. The Constitution initially made right to property, which includes land, a fundamental right; however, later this right was relegated to the position of a legal right but not a fundamental right. Practically, the doors of the courts have always been open for anyone whose land has been acquired by the government, particularly on the ground that the due process has not been followed—due process as procedure established by law mentioned in the Constitution but interpreted by the courts to incorporate the principles of due process, which include the principles of natural justice—and India has seen a large number of cases being taken right up to the Supreme Court.

The businesses, quite obviously, have continuously demanded the substantive and procedural law regarding land acquisition to be simple and without too much of appellate provisions, which is not in consonance with the spirit of rule of law and protection of legal rights practised in the country. The tension between the land rights and the demands of business to have easy access to land have very often led to serious litigation with heavy stakes involved. The purpose of the 2013 law on land acquisition is to reduce the scope for litigation and achieve balance between the land rights and demands of businesses. Only time will tell how far this law has been successful.

CASE STUDY

Delhi Development Authority v. Virender Lal Bahri, Supreme Court of India, 2019[26]

One of the greatest challenges in matters related to land acquisition is the interpretation of the law as the parties leave no stone unturned to get the law interpreted according to their convenience, once the facts are established and nothing can be done about the hard cold facts. Usually the stakes are high, and hence the effort is to play with the words of the law and try to convince the judge according to one's belief, or precisely what one would like the other to believe. This decision pertains to Section 24 of the 2013 Act, which repealed the 1894 Act. With the switching over to the new law of 2013, there were certain cases which were initiated under the old law of 1894 but were being handled under the new law.

This transition brings its own problems, and one of the general principles is to avoid any loss to the people if there is a conflict between the provisions of the old and new laws. Section 24 of the new law provides for some situations of lapsing of any process of land acquisition started under the old law, and a few portions relevant for this case read as follows:

> 24. Land acquisition process under Act No. 1 of 1894 shall be deemed to have lapsed in certain cases.
>
> (1) Notwithstanding anything contained in this Act, in any case of land acquisition proceedings initiated under the Land Acquisition Act, 1894 (1 of 1894),
>
> > (a) where no award under Section 11 of the said Land Acquisition Act has been made, then, all

---

[26] *Delhi Development Authority v. Virender Lal Bahri and others;* Supreme Court of India; 27 February 2019; Bench: R. F. Nariman, Vineet Saran, JJ.; Reported in 2019 Indlaw SC 249; Special Leave Petition (Civil) No. 37375 of 2016 with Special Leave Petition (Civil) No. 37372 of 2016, MA No. 1423 of 2017 in Civil Appeal No. 12247 of 2016, MA No. 1787 of 2017 in Civil Appeal No. 10210 of 2016, MA No. 1786 of 2017 in Civil Appeal No. 10207 of 2016, MA No. 45 of 2018 in Civil Appeal No. 6239 of 2017.

provisions of this Act relating to the determination of compensation shall apply; or

(b) where an award under said Section 11 has been made, then such proceedings shall continue under the provisions of the said Land Acquisition Act, as if the said Act has not been repealed.

(2) Notwithstanding anything contained in sub-section (1), in case of land acquisition proceedings initiated under the Land Acquisition Act, 1894, where an award under the said Section 11 has been made five years or more prior to the commencement of this Act but the physical possession of the land has not been taken or the compensation has not been paid the said proceedings shall be deemed to have lapsed and the appropriate Government, if it so chooses, shall initiate the proceedings of such land acquisition afresh in accordance with the provisions of this Act:

Provided that where an award has been made and compensation in respect of a majority of land holdings has not been deposited in the account of the beneficiaries, then, all beneficiaries specified in the notification for acquisition under Section 4 of the said Land Acquisition Act, shall be entitled to compensation in accordance with the provisions of this Act.[27]

To give a little more life to the old 1894 law to resolve the cases which had been initiated under that law so that the transition of law takes place smoothly, Section 24(1) begins with a non-obstante clause, that is, the word 'notwithstanding' which simply means despite the repealing of the old law and bringing in the new law, the old law shall be applicable in certain cases, and what are those cases has been discussed after that. Section 24(1) deals with compensation and Section 24(2) deals with lapsing of acquisition. The question

---

[27] Section 24, Right to Fair Compensation and Transparency in Land Acquisition, Rehabilitation and Resettlement Act, 2013.

is whether the proviso at the end of the Section applies to Section 24(1) or Section 24(2), or both.

The main purpose of the 2013 Act is to provide realistic and market rate compensation to landowners, and the proviso of this Section poses an obstacle if it is not interpreted in favour of the landowners. However, interpretation of any statute cannot be done in isolation and in vacuum but has to be done according to the context and in this particular statute the intention of the legislature is to compensate the landowners in a fair manner and make the executive work with alacrity so as not to let acquisition process linger on and thereby make the landowners suffer as their land is also acquired and compensation not really paid.

To take care of such situations, the legislature provided a certain time period, say five years, within which the process should have been completed otherwise the State is liable to make payment according to the new law. This all sounds fair and quite reasonable also, but interpretation by different courts in a different manner can have confusing results and create problems for both the landowners and the State. When challenged in an earlier case—*Tarun Pal v. Lieutenant Governor*[28]—the Delhi High Court had held that the proviso applies to Section 24(1)(b) and not to Section 24(2), but in 2018 the Supreme Court decided otherwise in the Delhi Metro Case[29] and held that the proviso governed Section 24(2) and not Section 24(1)(b).

---

[28] *Tarun Pal Singh and others v. Lieutenant Governor, Government of (NCT of Delhi) and others;* Delhi High Court; 21 May 2015; Bench: Badar Durrez Ahmed, Sanjeev Sachdeva, JJ.; Reported in 2015 Indlaw DEL 3511; W. P. (C) 8596/2014, W. P. (C) 2888/2014 & CM 14992/2014, 14994/2014 & 16227/2014 & CM 9997/2015, W. P. (C) 4839/2014 & CM 9662/2014 & CM 9998/2015, W. P. (C) 4462/2014 & CM 8898/2014 & CM 9999/2015, W. P. (C) 5559/2014 & CM 13785–13786/2014, W. P. (C) 6017/2014 & CM 17661/2014 & CM 10000/2015, W. P. (C) 6290/2014 & CM 15190/2014 & CM 9992/2015.

[29] *Delhi Metro Rail Corporation Limited v. Tarun Pal Singh and others;* Supreme Court of India; 15 November 2017; Bench: Arun Mishra, Mohan M. Shantanagoudar, JJ.; Reported in 2017 Indlaw SC 1265; 2018(1) SCALE 343; Civil Appeal No. 19356 of 2017 (Arising out of Slp (C) No. 25568/2016) with C. A. No. 19362/2017 Slp (C) No. 29265/2016, C. A. No. 19361/2017 Slp (C) No. 27420/2016, C. A. No. 19358/2017 Slp (C) No. 26346/2016, C. A. No. 19357/2017 Slp (C) No. 25569/2016, C. A. No. 19360/2017 Slp (C) No. 26348/2016, C. A. No. 19359/2017 Slp (C) No. 26347/2016, C. A. No. 19363/2017 Slp (C) No. 19846/2017, C. A. No. 19364/2017 Slp (C) No. 20653/2017, C. A. No. 19412/2017 Slp (C) No. 31886/2017, Diary No. 19957/2017.

There is clarity that as the 2018 decision is by the Supreme Court, it will prevail over the decision of the Delhi High Court, and for that matter the high court's decision had to be quashed in the light of new developments. This would however create a lot of problems as things which were settled for the last three years would be opened up and scrutinized afresh. In the instant case in 2019, the Supreme Court after detailed discussion came to the conclusion that the decision by the Supreme Court in 2018 was erroneous and the interpretation given by the Delhi High Court in 2015 was the correct one; however, as the bench strength in the Supreme Court in the decisions—2019 and 2018—is the same, that is, two judges, the 2018 decision cannot be overruled by the 2019 bench, and hence, the 2019 bench requested the Chief Justice to refer the matter to a five-judge bench which was already hearing a similar matter.

The interpretation of the statutes can be very tricky and this case highlights the uncertainty, confusion and chaos prevailing in the system, which does not facilitate proper decision-making. The sort of confusion is not at all conducive for proper business. Interestingly in 2019, the Supreme Court came to the conclusion on the basis of the fact that the new Land Acquisition Act of 2013 was a beneficial legislation and, hence, interpretation of any of the provisions of this statute should be done to further the basic purpose of the law. As two interpretations are possible, the more humane one, that is, the proviso applies to Section 24(1)(b) and not to Section 24(2), must be accepted. It is, therefore, quite evident that the provisions of the statute would be given proper meaning contextually and not at all with strict literal meaning being accepted on all occasions. The legislature can also step in and provide clarification as to what its intention was while making the law and let the clouds of doubt clear.

ENVIRONMENTAL CLEARANCE

The tussle between environment and development has been a very old story. To somehow aim for balancing between sustainability and infrastructure has been to a large extent theoretical. Practically, it has been experienced that the accepted normality in situations of environmental degradation is shifting to lower standards and there is a huge gap between what is being talked in the law, in the courts, etc., and the sad state of affairs at the ground level. A number of statutes have been enacted and enforced in India, and some of the important laws are: National Green Tribunal Act, 2010; Air (Prevention and Control of Pollution) Act, 1981; Water (Prevention and Control of Pollution) Act, 1974, etc.

Despite so many laws in India for the betterment of environmental protection and for penalizing the defaulters, the state of environment in India has been pathetic and, shockingly, the standards set for protecting environment have been flouted time and again. Infrastructure development and pollution in India have not been able to get along well. On more than one occasion, business units have not bothered even about the most fundamental aspects of sustainable development. Environmental adjudicating bodies have remained silent due to reasons best known to them causing irreparable harm and injury to the sociopolitical system. Non-compliance of the orders of the concerned tribunals has been a regular and routine matter, with companies obviously bothered about profits and their short-term gains, rather than the long-term perspective. The damages and fines awarded by the tribunals in India have been so minuscule as compared to the quantum ordered by courts in the developed world.

The Central Pollution Control Board (CPCB) was constituted in 1974 and currently provides technical expertise to the concerned ministries and promotes cleanliness and pollution control. It monitors air quality and collects data from different collection centres in different parts of the country, with focus on Delhi as the city has become notorious for its very high levels of pollution, and the obvious question has always been asked as to what the CPCB has been doing when pollution levels in Delhi have been so high. This has put extra pressure on the board to monitor air and water quality intensively in Delhi, which truly should be done in so many other parts of the country. The data collected by the board help in policy formulation and enforcement of different plans. Adjudication of disputes related to environment also gets the benefit of data for objective decision-making.

The National Green Tribunal (NGT), which was established under the National Green Tribunal Act, 2010, is the highest tribunal regarding environment matters and has been given the mandate to take care of issues related to the sustainability of forests and natural resources along with development in general, and infrastructure development in particular. The primary purpose of this tribunal is to adjudicate matters related to environment protection, conservation of forests and also to look into the matters pertaining to award of compensation to people who are relocated because of construction and also to take care of their rehabilitation. The scope of this tribunal is quite wide and it includes all the laws related to pollution of all types (mainly air and water pollution), forests and biodiversity.

The NGT Act of 2010 repealed the National Environment Tribunal Act, 1995, and the National Environment Appellate Authority Act, 1997. Deciding matters related to environment in a speedy manner, and also effectively, has been the foremost goal of establishment of the NGT; however, it has been experienced that it has not been as effective as was envisaged and most of the matters involving high stakes are appealed in the Supreme Court, and many a time these orders have been stayed in the Supreme Court along with not very pleasing remarks. Sometimes, it appears as a toothless tiger and has also raised the issue of its relevance in the changed circumstances when infrastructure development must take place at a very rapid pace to cater to the rising aspirations of the people of India.

There is hardly any time to go into long hearings and thereafter get everything shifted to the Supreme Court. For several important matters, to some observers, the NGT appears as a hurdle in speedy decision-making and increases uncertainty in the system.[30] Since the establishment of the NGT, there has not been any substantial improvement in environmental conditions in the country, and Delhi particularly has become excessively polluted as is evident almost every year post-Diwali at the onset of winter. Steps taken by the NGT have not yielded any desired results which led to the constant monitoring of even firecrackers by the Supreme Court. This is most unsatisfactory and requires immediate attention to tackle the problem and make the tribunal effective.

---

[30] Joyeeta Basu, 'SC's Sterlite Ruling Puts Question Mark on NGT', *Deccan Chronicle* (2019, 20 February). Available at https://www.deccanchronicle.com/nation/current-affairs/200219/scs-sterlite-ruling-puts-question-mark-on-ngt.html (accessed on 24 April 2019).

CASE STUDY

Tamil Nadu Pollution Control Board v. Sterlite Industries India, Supreme Court of India, 2019[31]

It is a case in which the dispute has been passed from one judicial forum to another, and there is confusion galore about the mandate of the quasi-judicial bodies and regulatory institutions. Briefly the facts are: Sterlite was operating a copper smelter plant at Thoothukudi in Tamil Nadu since 1997. All the requisite clearances were obtained from different clearance agencies in the state and at the centre. With ever-increasing awareness about pollution and the active intervention by the judiciary, the Supreme Court constituted a committee in 2004 to evaluate the method of managing hazardous waste. The committee did not approve of the system at the company. The Tamil Nadu Pollution Control Board (TNPCB), despite the committee's disapproval, granted its conditional consent to operate the plant.

A number of petitions were filed in the Madras High Court by environment protection groups and also the local residents complained of medical problems due to emissions from the plant. The high court quashed the clearances and the TNPCB took a strict view and directed the company to stop its operations. Sterlite moved the NGT for stay of TNPCB order and got a decision in its favour. A number of orders were passed by the TNPCB, the Madras High Court, the NGT, Tamil Nadu government and the Supreme Court. Heavy lobbying took place by bringing in business consultants and environmentalists by the company at all levels—central government, state government and the State and CPCBs.

Also, the company started a well-oiled campaign to clear its name in the media, at Indian and global platforms, research papers impacting the regulatory bodies and talking about the

---

[31] *Tamil Nadu Pollution Control Board v. Sterlite Industries India Limited and others;* Supreme Court of India; 18 February 2019; Bench: R. F. Nariman, Navin Sinha, JJ.; Reported in 2019 Indlaw SC 195; Civil Appeal Nos. 4763–4764 of 2013 with Civil Appeal Nos. 8773–8774 of 2013, Civil Appeal Nos. 9542–9543 of 2013, Civil Appeal No. 5782 of 2014, Civil Appeal Nos. 1552–1554 of 2019, Civil Appeal No. 23 of 2019, Civil Appeal No. 1582 of 2019.

role of judiciary in the process of development along with taking into account the environmental concerns. Similar efforts were made by the NGOs, environmental experts, legal thinkers writing about the role of judiciary and judicial review, the government at the centre and in the state of Tamil Nadu, and somehow bringing the troubles faced by the local residents in limelight so as to have a meaningful debate with two extremes set—crony capitalism exploiting mining resources at the cost of environmental degradation and human misery on the one hand and human rights of individuals, environmental protection and sustainable development on the other.

It became quite obvious that the role of the NGT had been to allow the mining company to operate as the tribunal was usually passing orders to that effect on almost all occasions, whenever such a matter was presented before it for adjudication. In April and May 2018, the TNPCB and Tamil Nadu government had passed a total of six orders directing the Sterlite not to continue operations. These six orders were appealed by a composite appeal in the NGT. The fundamental question to be answered is regarding the mandate and jurisdiction of the NGT as far as the issue of judicial review of executive orders is concerned. There has been a view, though not widely accepted, that the NGT has almost the same powers of a high court, and hence it has the authority to judicially review the executive orders.

This view has not been accepted by the Supreme Court. After detailed discussion and analysis of a large number of cases cited by lawyers from both the sides, the Supreme Court held that it would be absolutely erroneous to assume that the NGT—a creation of a statute—has all the powers of high courts, which has been established according to the provisions of the Constitution of India. The Supreme Court did not decide the case on the merits, as the short question before it was about the power of judicial review and, thus, maintainability of appeal filed by Sterlite at the NGT. The Supreme Court categorically stated that the NGT did not have jurisdiction in this matter and should not have entertained the composite appeal.

If it had done so on the basis of certain grounds, doctrine of necessity, being an expert body to hear environmental matters, absence of an appellate authority, etc., then the NGT was undoubtedly stretching its jurisdiction beyond permissible legal limits, as established by the parent statute. As no appeal lies in the NGT against the six challenged orders by the composite appeal, the Supreme Court observed that Sterlite was free to move the high court for desired relief. This decision of the Supreme Court has been a big blow to the stature and position of the NGT which has to be realistic in its approach and work within the set legal framework. For business and infrastructure development, presence of multiple forums can be reassuring and provide several options; however, it all brings in high levels of uncertainty and results in sheer waste of time, effort, money and opportunities as, truly speaking, matters with very high stakes are seldom accepted by parties till the time the final order is pronounced by the Supreme Court.

KEY TAKEAWAYS

- *Land acquisition:* The biggest challenge in infrastructure and PPP projects is land acquisition. It should not be taken for granted. Despite all the support and help of the government, it may take a very long time. Private businesses must be extra careful about it.

- *Environment:* The issues of environment can make or mar a PPP project. Even if the project is otherwise viable and sustainable, environment issues may be raised by anyone, who is not at all related to the project or suffering from it. Executives should be aware of these issues and must try to comply with all statutory and regulatory requirements.

- *Technology:* With the technology frontier being pushed forward every day, even the latest technologies become obsolete quite fast. Business executives ought to update themselves on the newest developments. Substantial investing in R&D will give handsome dividends.

Chapter 5
FUNDING AND LEGAL FRAMEWORK

Infrastructure is usually a big ticket item requiring heavy investment, which is not always possible for the governments and that is why there is a need for private participation. Governments can provide the required funds through budget allocation; however, as the aspirations of the people keep rising, the financial resources are inadequate for the demands of the society. The budget allocation has to be done by the governments in democratic countries ostensibly for the heads which are directly linked with socio-economic justice, equality, environmental issues, agriculture, education, health, sanitation, etc., and other heads which are critical for the peaceful existence of the country, such as defence, internal law and order, administration, revenue, etc. In this list, a new airport or a bullet train does not fit in and will always look the odd man out.

As we have discussed earlier, good existing infrastructure is always helpful in conducting business—commercial and social—and regular upgradation and maintenance are necessary to meet the demands of tomorrow. Just like Rome was not built in a day, infrastructure projects cannot be completed in a jiffy; they require long-term planning, commitment, financial viability and abiding interest. This is the biggest dilemma for governments in most of the countries as to where to put the money in—in essential areas which cannot be neglected, or if neglected or given a secondary treatment are bound to adversely impact the political future of the party or coalition in power; or in infrastructure development projects, which undoubtedly are needed by the country, but do not fall in the category of 'urgent and essential'.

Primarily because of this reason, the governments are not able to allocate sufficient funds for infrastructure projects and, thus, these projects become heavily dependent on funding other than from the budgetary allocation. Some of the infrastructure projects do get support from the government in the form of proper earmarking in the budget as these projects are essential for the people and might have been in demand for a very long time. The state-owned enterprises, also known as PSUs, can also fund certain infrastructure projects particularly in their domain of expertise and business. Very often the PSUs are able to amalgamate the best of the government and private advantages, positioning themselves uniquely, to achieve the desired goals in terms of project management and technological advances.

Despite suffering from the public perception of being inefficient, many PSUs in India and elsewhere also have demonstrated fantastic strides in commercial success. This is no mean achievement for the PSUs which are working within the extremely strict and demanding legal requirements, fundamental rights in the Constitution, right to information, scrutiny by various central authorities, etc., expected from the state enterprises as contradistinguished with private business which is not burdened with many such onerous legal conditions. It makes sense for these PSUs to invest back the surplus cash into the task of new infrastructure creation and thus contributing to nation building. Often there are a few members from the government on the board of these PSUs which makes it possible for the government to have certain indirect control on the decision-making process at the very top level.

Sometimes, the government of the day blatantly tries to control the entire decision-making aggressively without bothering about the corporate governance norms and the niceties of good governance. To a certain extent, infrastructure funding can be managed through the PSUs; however, depending on the demands for new infrastructure, private funding has to be made available to bridge the gap between the high demand and low supply of funds. This funding can come either from domestic players or from foreign investors. Rarely it will come from individuals as it entails very high and avoidable risk. The private funding, therefore, comes usually from banks, financial institutions, SPVs, lending entities created by pooling money from individuals or families with ready excessive cash available.

International institutions such as the World Bank, the Asian Development Bank and the International Monetary Fund, fund various infrastructure projects to make the world a better place to live in and also to take care of the upliftment of people in different jurisdictions; however, all this funding comes with strings attached, chiefly in the form of adhering to respecting the fundamental human rights, democratic norms, no child labour, no or minimum negative impact on the environment, practising austerity and surely promising to pay back with interest, howsoever low it may be. For extremely poor countries with hardly any other source of investment, funding from these institutions is the only source for money, and very often the governments in these countries are not able to honour the commitment with some of the conditions mentioned earlier. Such a situation results in a debt trap making the country heavily dependent on foreign investors, which is not at all an enviable position for a sovereign nation.

CASE STUDY

Banks and Financial Institutions: The IL&FS Case, 2018

For the last 25 years or so, infrastructure projects in India have been able to attract financing from foreign investors as well as banks in India and other investors in India. There has been great enthusiasm at the turn of the century and the early parts of the first decade regarding financing PPP projects; however, with the passage of time, due to certain reasons—mostly uncertainties about the continuity of policies with change in governments—the returns on investment were not as expected by the investors which led to waning of investment by the private investors. There was visible reluctance on the part of the banks and other financial institutions to invest in PPP projects in India and the reason primarily has been policy paralysis on the political front and increasingly tightening of norms for operation for bankers and key functionaries in financial institutions.

Private investors are wary of investing in greenfield projects due to a number of obstacles faced by such projects, especially various clearances by the government. Most of the banks in India, predominately the nationalized banks, have burnt their fingers by taking keen interest in PPP projects and supporting them but not able to recover the amount lent, forget about the interest, on several occasions. Specialized organizations dealing in infrastructure financing like the IL&FS Ltd have also not been doing well and the IL&FS completely failed in the latter part of 2018.

It was created about three decades back to invest in PPP projects and has been considered to be the pioneer financial institution to do so. It had the backing of several foreign investors and also some Indian investors. Interestingly, it has been the brainchild of a few bankers and financial experts in the country who knew the financial system like the back of their hands. In 2018, it had unpaid debt of roughly $13 billion and there was no possible manner in which it could have paid that sum of money. Some of the experts were of the opinion that the crisis created by the IL&FS was almost like the end of the country's romance with PPPs and the idea of funding these projects through private funds was finished.

Conceptually, PPPs are dependent on the concessionaire—the private party—making the arrangement for funds and in case of the banks and financial institutions not willing to support it, the matter comes back to square one, that is, the government has to arrange for the funds. There are a number of stories leading to a number of investigations into the wheelers and dealers of funding the PPPs and thus gaining the prime spots in infrastructure projects and thereby attracting immense attention of almost everyone—construction companies, architects, media persons, political masters, bureaucrats, public in general, etc. Money makes the mare go, and that's why legal and regulatory action on the funding agencies has been more than enough to decelerate, or stop in many cases, the ongoing journey of infrastructure projects.

The legal framework in India has been evolving and the National Company Law Tribunal (NCLT), constituted in 2016 and established under the Companies Act, 2013, has been the main quasi-judicial body adjudicating issues related to companies including insolvency and winding up. Matters related to the IL&FS are pending in the NCLT, where serious questions have been raised regarding the working of the IL&FS and its relationship with its auditors and chartered accountants. The Ministry of Corporate Affairs has been highly critical of their working and cosy relationship which might have prompted them to ignore blatant violations of financial and accounting norms while garnering and monitoring funds for the PPP projects.

What was the extent of personal benefits accrued by the individuals working for the IL&FS and the auditing firms may never be able to be known to the public as a good number of transactions were on the sly and unrecorded. The auditors did not check the lender about the obvious non-feasible lending, which easily can be concluded either as negligence or collusion. The IL&FS worked with a fairly large number of intra-group companies, with borrowing and lending from one company to another in the same group being routine, and usually without substantial reasoning to do so. Many a time, the Reserve Bank of India (RBI) norms were prima facie violated without compunction. The government is asserting in the NCLT that the previous board of the IL&FS and the auditors are guilty of professional misconduct and failed to perform their fiduciary duty.

It was not only the failure of IL&FS officers and its auditors but also the failure of credit rating agencies which were not able to anticipate and gauge the financial troubles so many companies under the IL&FS umbrella were going through. The RBI was quite critical of the role of these agencies which could not foresee the credit risks and did not take any timely action.[32] It was only when the failure of the IL&FS had come out in the open, or a little before that, the credit rating agencies downgraded the ratings suddenly, resulting panic in the market. That is precisely what has to be avoided with the presence of rating agencies which are supposed to keep their antennas sharp and catch the slightest of the possible signals and make corrections in the ratings accordingly.

If this was not done in a similar manner and sudden ups and downs took place in the market, lenders and investors are as good as without any support of the rating agencies. Ratings going slightly up and down are like forecasting seismic activity in an earthquake-prone area. There is no advantage of getting to know from seismologists about the occurrence of an earthquake when all the buildings have already collapsed and there is chaos all around. The seismologists should be able to predict an earthquake when there are sure signs appearing for an expert, but not for an unskilled person. In the same way, the rating agencies ought to spot stress in the system and timely warn the concerned persons to mitigate the damage.

Soft enforcement of corporate governance norms do not take care of conflict of interests of individuals straddling from one

---

[32] *ET Now News*, 'RBI Flays Credit Rating Agencies for Being Late in Identifying IL&FS Crisis,' 8 March 2019. Available at https://www.timesnownews.com/business-economy/economy/article/rbi-governor-shaktikanta-das-flays-credit-rating-agencies-for-being-late-in-identifying-ilfs-crisis/379038 (accessed on 24 April 2019).

company to another, and from one role to another. This is particularly true about the rating agencies which are well known for hiring common individuals both for the rating and other functions such as market research, risk management, lending and consultancy in particular. The RBI does not approve of such a practice and strongly censures common individuals manning key positions, which makes it almost impossible to avoid conflict of interests. The Securities and Exchange Board of India (SEBI) has also an important role to play as the credit rating agencies are registered with it. The SEBI was created by the SEBI Act, 1992, as a statutory body, though as a non-statutory body it was established in 1988.

It is responsible for protecting investors' interests in securities by regulating the securities market. It performs legislative, executive and judicial functions, all in a quasi-fashion. Its decisions can be appealed in the appellate body called Securities Appellate Tribunal (SAT), and thereafter in the Supreme Court. The SEBI has been actively promoting corporate governance norms, especially disclosure and transparency so that accountability can be fixed. The manner in which the IL&FS had conducted its business, which brought its downfall, can hardly be worth emulating and it is scandalous that despite the strict guidelines of the SEBI and the RBI, and other mandatory norms to be complied with, top management in the IL&FS was able to 'manage' the show for such a long time.

LEGAL FRAMEWORK

For infrastructure development, the legal framework for finance mobilization, usage, repayment and related issues is guided by the broad legal environment and hence is affected by and affects the business environment. For decades, borrowing money in India has been a big problem as there was always crunch of resources and seeking adequate finances for any infrastructure project was a nightmare. There was opacity in the system which led to sanctioning loans of a certain chosen companies due to their prominence in the market and ability to network with lenders and bankers. Government control on sanctioning of funds, directly or indirectly, also helped in highly successful infrastructure companies in getting more than adequate funds, whereas newer companies and companies without any connections in the decision-making circles were hardly able to get loans sanctioned from the lenders.

During the days of Licence-Permit Raj, lending was mostly in the hands of public sector banks and government institutions. For so many decades, there hardly had been any accountability and very often loss-making infrastructure companies were able to get more and more funds, simply on the ground of calling it restructuring of loans and making it possible for the company to do business. Of late, numerous changes have been made in the legal framework to make the borrowers who have not been doing well to be held accountable, and to make resources available for companies and individuals who have the zeal and enthusiasm to work hard and do something profitable with borrowed money while doing something good for the society.

CASE STUDY

ArcelorMittal India Private Limited v. Satish Kumar Gupta, Supreme Court of India, 2018[33]

Steel has been an integral part of infrastructure development for about two centuries. Production of steel indigenously had been the plank of nationalists in India so as to reduce dependence on foreign steel and Indian steel manufacturers

---

[33] *ArcelorMittal India Private Limited v. Satish Kumar Gupta and others;* Supreme Court of India; 4 October 2018; Bench: R.F. Nariman, Indu Malhotra, JJ.; Reported in: 2018 Indlaw SC 919; Civil Appeal Nos. 9402–9405 of 2018 with Civil Appeal No. 9582 of 2018, Civil Appeal No. of 2018, Diary No. 35253 of 2018, Civil Appeal No. of 2018, Diary No. 33971 of 2018.

have been successful in this endeavour to a large extent. But steel manufacturing requires heavy initial investment and the break-even takes place after a very long period of time. When the Indian economy opened up for private investment, steel and cement were two sectors which saw huge investments, as these are essential for the infrastructure expansion in any meaningful manner. However, with the global trade being the norm post-WTO formation, it became possible for manufacturers of excessive quantity of steel to dump it in the international market at very low rates. China, with the advantage of economies of scale and low manufacturing cost, has been able to capture the global steel market resulting in crashing of steel prices.

Low prices made it unprofitable for many steel mills in so many countries and Indian companies also faced the heat. Essar Steel India Limited (Essar) promoted and managed by the billionaire Ruia family had fallen on bad days and was looking for any legal possibility to wriggle out of the bankruptcy. The company had seen many evil days and was on the verge of bankruptcy at the turn of the century and faced serious difficulties time and again. With the enactment of the IBC, 2016, the legal proceedings became quite tough and straightforward.[34]

In 2017, Essar had to pay about ₹50,000 crores (about $7 billion at the current rate of exchange) to the creditors, mainly State Bank of India and the Standard Chartered Bank. With hardly any possibility of making the payment or even a proper repayment plan, Essar could not escape the clutches of IBC, 2016. The NCLT at Ahmedabad appointed Satish Kumar Gupta (Gupta) as the interim resolution professional (IRP) according to IBC. According to the procedure laid down in IBC, Gupta advertised for potential resolution applicants. ArcelorMittal—the merged entity after the merger of Arcelor Steel and Mittal Steel—and Numetal submitted expressions

---

[34] Vishwanath Nair, 'Has the Ruia Family Finally Lost Essar Steel?' *Bloomberg*, 8 September 2018. Available at https://www.bloombergquint.com/insolvency/has-the-ruia-family-finally-lost-essar-steel#gs.02dkgg (accessed on 24 April 2019).

of interest. Gupta, thereafter, published an RfP for submitting resolution plans.

The duration of the insolvency resolution process was extended to the maximum time period of 270 days, that is, till the end of April 2018. Both ArcelorMittal and Numetal made the submission of their respective resolution plans. Gupta found both the parties—ArcelorMittal and Numetal—ineligible due to conflict of interests of promoters and backroom manoeuvring to gain control of Essar. Both ArcelorMittal and Numetal challenged IRP Gupta's order at the adjudicating authority, NCLT. In between, fresh resolution plans were submitted by ArcelorMittal, Numetal and another company Vedanta. In a detailed order, the NCLT upheld the decision of the IRP and remanded the matter to the Committee of Creditors (CoC). Again, both the companies appealed against the NCLT order in the National Company Law Appellate Tribunal (NCLAT). The CoC disqualified both ArcelorMittal and Numetal on different grounds.

The NCLAT did not give any favourable order and passed the buck to the CoC for early disposal of the matter and directed that the number of days the appeal was pending should not be included in the period of 270 days. It is against the order of the NCLAT that both ArcelorMittal and Numetal appealed in the Supreme Court. It is quite disturbing to note the ease with which the number of days a matter is pending in appeal can be subtracted from the stipulated maximum time period of 270 days, which is the extended period after the initially scheduled time of 180 days. The purpose of fixing the time period is to make the process take place speedily without being derailed in multiple appeals and interim applications.

However, not counting the days of appeal shall raise a question mark in the prompt decision-making envisioned in the IBC. The only argument and solace is 'better late than never' and that 'at least the things are moving, even if at a slow pace' and 'thank God for small mercies'. To a certain extent, there is merit in accepting the things the way they are taking place as highly ambitious plans may not be possible to be executed within strict time limits and that too when the insolvency proceedings are in its nascent stage in India. ArcelorMittal stated in the court that Numetal was a shell company and should not be allowed to take part in the resolution proceedings.[35]

During the arguments, a mesh of companies controlling each other, or having some stake in each other came to fore, and it was also brought to the notice of the Supreme Court that Numetal was promoted by a member of the Ruia family, which had promoted and controlled Essar. So, in brief, it was a desperate attempt by the Ruia family to somehow—indirectly and discreetly—retain the control over Essar in the garb of a resolution plan under the IBC. This should not be allowed, as any such move would defeat the basic purpose of IBC. Ironically, Numetal's counsel stated the very old settled principle that a company is a distinct legal entity and an artificial legal person, very different from its shareholders and promoters.

This appears to be a frantic attempt in saving the company Numetal from being disqualified as the entire purpose of IBC is to go deep into the working of the company and find out who the real actors controlling the company are. It is, in a way, lifting the corporate veil in a statutory manner, as provided in the IBC. Highly technical arguments aimed at legal hairsplitting—and that's precisely the job of a lawyer—were made but in the process, the counsel on both the sides were somehow ignoring the complete picture and were simply focusing in on the portion favourable to them. This practice is not conducive to the very high standards set by exemplary legal practitioners in bringing out the complete picture and, thereafter, arguing on the merits of the case, using sophisticated legalese and finesse.

The IBC was amended in 2017 to add the phrase 'persons acting in concert' which was basically done to catch hold of individuals who acted together to negate the provisions of IBC and were difficult to be nailed using obvious and direct

---

[35] *NDTV Profit*, 'NuMetal A "Shell Company," Can't Bid For Essar Steel, Says ArcelorMittal,' 13 September 2018. Available at https://www.ndtv.com/business/numetal-a-shell-company-cant-bid-for-essar-steel-says-arcelormittal-1916226 (accessed on 24 April 2019).

evidence. Circumstantial and indirect evidence is the only option and has to be intelligently produced in a court of law by connecting the relevant dots, which are not apparent to the untrained eyes. In 2017, the IBC was amended to rope in all the persons who were behind the submission of resolution plan, even if they were not conspicuous formally on paper. Thus, the amended IBC referred to the de facto position to find out the persons in control of the resolution plan.

The Supreme Court observed that the amended IBC must be interpreted purposely and not literally so as to give a proper meaning and interpretation of the law. A shareholder undoubtedly is separate from the company; however, in case the company has been incorporated by that shareholder or shareholders with the wrongful purpose of taking control of the bankrupt entity through submission of a resolution plan, well settled and literal meaning will facilitate the dubious design of incorporating the company for a mala fide motive. This is the bounden duty of the courts not to allow it to happen. The 'see-through provision'—as to who are the real persons controlling the activity—has to be recognized and given due importance while interpreting the statute.

Detailed analysis of the facts of the case made the Supreme Court to conclude that Numetal as a company was controlled by the Ruias and was incorporated with the sole purpose of submitting the resolution plan clandestinely by the family. Regarding ArcelorMittal, the Supreme Court came to the conclusion that with the help of a big web of companies investing and controlling each other, with everything ultimately leading to L. N. Mittal, the chairman and CEO of the company, and having certain stakes in Essar, it could not be considered to be absolutely independent and unrelated to the company undergoing the insolvency process. Thus, the Supreme Court upheld the decision of the NCLAT that both the companies were rightly disqualified.

Some more time was given to submit fresh resolution plans after taking care of all the glitches pointed out in the court order—mainly to pay dues and get the 'defaulter' tag removed—and if no plan was acceptable according to law, Essar would go into liquidation. Later, in March 2019, the NCLT allowed the resolution plan of ArcelorMittal, which found favour with the tribunal.[36] Some of the lenders, though, are not satisfied with the decision. Essar and the Standard Chartered Bank have already stated that they will appeal in the NCLAT. Eventually, the lenders are interested in getting back their money and ArcelorMittal made a decent proposal according to some lenders. Essar insolvency can be a test case as this is one of the 'Dirty Dozen' notified by the RBI.

SMART CITIES, PPP AND FUNDING

In 2015, the Smart Cities Mission[37] (SCM) was started with the target of upgrading 100 cities in the country. It is very well known that the number of people living in cities is rising and, hence, the problems of urbanization have led to poor quality of living in cities with health and hygiene being one of the major issues, besides sanitation, roads, power, water, housing, etc. All this has to be provided keeping in mind concerns related to environment and ecological balance. Even with the best of intentions and greatest of the willingness to do something good, continuous flow of adequate funds is required to get things completed and one of the biggest challenges in upgrading the cities in India was, and will remain, availability of financial resources.

The government had decided to involve the private businesses in this task and get funding, as well as the latest technology and managerial inputs. All this has to be done within the

---

[36] Vishal Dutta, 'NCLT Ahmedabad Clears ArcelorMittal's ₹42,000 Crore Resolution Plan for Essar Steel,' *Economic Times*, 9 March 2019. Available at https://economictimes.indiatimes.com/industry/indl-goods/svs/steel/nclt-ahmedabad-clears-arcelormittals-rs-42000-crore-resolution-plan-for-essar-steel/articleshow/68321722.cms (accessed on 24 April 2019).
[37] http://smartcities.gov.in/content/ (accessed on 24 April 2019).

framework of the Constitution and administrative law, and with too many political forces acting in almost all the directions. It is easier said than done as getting the available resources channelized in one single direction, particularly having only one centre of power and authority, rather than splitting that centre in more than one and thereby creating an opportunity to have conflicts, is the biggest challenge. It was decided that the central government will grant about ₹100 crore every year, and the state governments and the urban local bodies will contribute an equal sum for each city.

For this purpose, an SPV was registered under the Companies Act, 2013, which is a distinct corporate entity to plan and implement the project in different cities rather than going through the route of municipal bodies already existing.[38] However, there have been certain common functionaries, especially the officers heading the SPVs and the local municipal bodies, which might in the long run be creating conflict of interests, but it is important in the beginning to have alignment of actions and synergy in which the new entity and the old municipal bodies work together. The basic idea is to create smart cities which are ready for the future in terms of providing better housing, workplaces, green spaces, parks, places for recreation, etc., along with the scope for further expansion.

Cutting-edge technology, including artificial intelligence, is envisaged to be used for power distribution and consumption; waste disposal, using the waste and sewage for making manure; recycling of water, glass, metals, etc.; minimizing the use of fossil fuel, and in general providing a far superior environment

---

[38] G. Seetharaman, 'Smart Cities Mission Is Still Very Much a Work in Progress Post Three Years of Its Launch,' *Economic Times*, 9 June 2018. Available at https://economictimes.indiatimes.com/news/economy/infrastructure/smart-cities-mission-is-still-very-much-a-work-in-progress-post-three-years-of-its-launch/articleshow/64523035.cms (accessed on 24 April 2019).

for living, as to what people are experiencing currently and try to make the best use of the technology as its frontiers are pushed further. As far as the SPVs are concerned, there is a view of certain observers that instead of strengthening the already existing municipal bodies, the central government had created a parallel body, making the cities dependent on the central government for financing and several approvals, indirectly eroding the fundamental concept of local self-government.

There is, however, a counterargument that had it been so easy and simple for the local municipal bodies to do such a thing, they would have already done it as no one had stopped them from doing anything good so far. There's definitely some slowdown in release of funds by the central government for the SCM, but these may be teething problems and a lot depends on the initiative taken by a particular city and the state government to arrange their contribution to the SPV rather than depending heavily on the central governments contribution, as the long-term solution is for making the city self-dependent and plan for its growth and development in a unique manner, keeping in mind its history and heritage, geographical location, distinctive characteristics, special needs, rather than simply copying one template followed by any particular city which might have been successful.

It is quite certain that one size doesn't fit all when city planning and development are under consideration. With the use of technology, a lot of data has been collected and which is proving to be of great value while making the broader plan and thereafter in designing specific facilities.[39] The real-time

---

[39] Arindam Guha, 'Smart Cities and PPPs: Why Data Is the New Currency,' *Financial Express*, 12 January 2018. Available at https://www.financialexpress.com/opinion/smart-cities-and-ppps-why-data-is-the-new-currency/1011514/ (accessed on 24 April 2019).

data and the use of data analytics tools have made decision-making more scientific and objective, and it is truly a boon for the planners to counter the often whimsical and unreasonable demands of political masters of constructing a building or road somewhere, it simply does not make any sense except appeasing the voters in that area.

FUNDING FOR EPC AND HAM PROJECTS

The Engineering, Procurement and Construction (EPC) projects require the contractor to complete the work and hand it over to the government. Typically, these projects are such contracting arrangements which make the EPC contractor accountable for all the activities. However, hybrid annuity model (HAM) projects are a mix of EPC contracts and BOT. These are different models of PPP projects where the government contributes something besides approvals and clearances in the form of project cost. Under the EPC model, almost the entire risk remains with the government as it is completely funding the project and is simply looking forward to awarding the contract to an engineering company which can complete the job according to the technical specifications and at the most reasonable cost, which is known as the lowest bid, that is, L1.

Usually, procurement of material is done by the government and most of the clearances, including the highly contentious land and environmental clearances, are also the responsibility of the government. The contracting company is awarded the contract to get the benefit of its core competence in engineering and bringing in the latest in technology and management skills. Simply put, financial risk for the private company is minimum as compared to the HAM projects. The major problem of EPC model for the government is huge financial risk and also a great deal of uncertainty in making the payments due to varied interpretations of the escalation clauses, time and cost overrun, legal remedial actions in arbitration and court cases, which go on and on for several years and sometimes decades.

To let the private parties share some of the financial burden as is there in EPC contracts, the government used the BOT annuity model commonly in a good number of PPP projects. The government is not responsible for making the full payments till the time the contract completes the work, operates it for a certain pre-decided time and thereafter receives payment from the government after definite time intervals according to the understanding between the two parties as mentioned in the CA. Clearly, this model requires a private party to invest a considerable sum of money for a longish period of time, and thereafter to wait for the government to make the payment, which at times may get clouded in a lot of disputes, controversies and conflicts resulting in arbitrations according to contractual clauses and PIL.

Huge uncertainty in getting the payment in time, and in totality, is many a time dissuading for private players to take the avoidable risk and rather prefer to go for a smaller, but certain, profits. This again tilts in favour of EPC contracts. In another method, known as the BOT toll model, the government does not make any payment to the contractor, as the contractor is supposed to collect toll on the roads and highways constructed over a pretty long period of time—usually 20–30 years—and get a reasonable ROI made in the beginning and also in maintaining the roads and highways for the period of time as mentioned in the CA.

This condition is typically characterized by high levels of uncertainty as the conditions of business may change even in a period of five years which may be very different from what had been assumed at the time of signing the agreement. Changes in political, economic and legal environment impact the projects the most. These uncertainties somehow do not encourage the private players to commit themselves for the long periods of time as CAs require. It is quite natural that the private companies would like to break even and then make profits at the earliest and would not like to live in uncertainty. Therefore, the BOT toll model is not being heavily favoured by the private companies.

To promote the PPP model, the government encouraged HAM projects and promised to pay 40 per cent of the project cost in the first five years, and the remaining 60 per cent of the completion of the project as variable annuity amount. However, the private player is expected to raise 60 per cent of the project cost also in the first five years as loans or equity. For the highways and road projects, the private players do not get any right to collect tolls, as this right remains with the government or a public body. There is sharing of financial risk by the government, but borrowing the money from banks and financial institutions is a problem for private players after the tightening of lending norms, and strict action on NPAs with the changing legal environment primarily after the enactment of IBC, 2016.

The government is trying to push the HAM projects to revive a large number of held up projects but the private players have shown their reluctance despite assurances by the government of timely payments of the annuity amount, speedy clearances, effective dispute resolution, almost zero bureaucratic meddling, giving complete freedom to proceed with the project in a fully professional manner, least political interference, simple and manageable terms and conditions for technology transfer, access to loans, etc. It has been observed that the private companies have somehow lost the confidence in very long-term projects and are eager to take up wieldy and time-bound projects to make a decent profit at the end of the day.

The locking in resources, mainly men, material and money, for long periods of time ends up in huge loans, which need to be serviced routinely. Even the ordinary interest payments can be killing for a private company if revenue streams are blocked. It often results in Catch-22 situation for the private companies as the resources are blocked and until and unless the projects are completed, they are not at all in a position to make the timely payments, and for restarting a stalled project, there is a dire need of financial infusion. Banks and other lenders are not willing to put in money in HAM projects,[40] and that is primarily the reason why private companies are also favouring EPC model.[41]

KEY TAKEAWAYS

- *Risk sharing:* The main advantage of PPP projects is sharing of risk between the public and private parties. The rights and duties of the two are put in black and white in the CAs and the risk is usually according to the relative bargaining power of the parties (inversely proportional); however, the State usually tries to shift

---

[40] Rajesh Naidu, 'Banks Not Too Keen on Funding HAM Projects as NPAs Swell,' *The Economic Times*, 28 September 2018. Available at https://economictimes.indiatimes.com/industry/banking/finance/banking/banks-not-too-keen-on-funding-ham-projects-as-npas-swell/articleshow/65988343.cms (accessed on 25 April 2019).
[41] Rajesh Naidu, 'Construction Cos Prefer Pure EPC Jobs to Annuity Projects,' *The Economic Times*, 20 March 2019. Available at https://economictimes.indiatimes.com/markets/stocks/news/construction-cos-prefer-pure-epc-jobs-to-annuity-projects/articleshow/68490572.cms (accessed on 25 April 2019).

the heavy burden on the private party. This approach practically does not work in the long run as has been experienced in India forcing the government to be more participative in funding the projects.

- *Borrowing money gets difficult:* It is not easy to borrow money as investors, domestic and foreign, look for superior ROI. Infrastructure projects seek huge borrowings, which cost a lot in a tight financial market. In case of upward and downward swings in the market conditions, the borrowing is affected. Private players should not make assumptions for the future when the market is going very strong as the situation may change drastically with weak markets. They must plan keeping the worst case scenario in mind.

- *Changing legal framework:* The dynamic legal framework for financial markets, investments, borrowing and lending, and business in general can simply make projects come to a grinding halt. Being optimistic is good and positive; however, over-optimism leading to sheer recklessness is not practical. Taking legal environment and proceedings casually may be self-destructive at times. Legal framework is capable of changing in the blink of an eye and, hence, must be taken with due seriousness.

Chapter 6

JUDICIARY AND INFRASTRUCTURE

In the present scheme of things in India, the judiciary is supposed to be, and perceived to be, the strongest of the three arms of government: the legislature, executive and judiciary. The judicial system in India, currently, has been the result of a heavy mix of thousands of years of civilization in India; however, there is undoubtedly the dominance of the colonial hangover of the British rule in the last couple of centuries. Most of the basic laws in the country, presently, have been the result of the legislative exercise initiated in the latter half of the 19th century—after the first war of independence in 1857, called mutiny by the British—with the most noticeable examples being the Indian Penal Code, 1860, the Indian Evidence Act, 1872, and the Indian Contract Act, 1872.

The control by the British Empire over the people of India continued in the early parts of the 20th century, but the things changed dramatically when India became independent in 1947 and the primary function of the law witnessed a paradigm shift from being an instrument in the 'Police State' to that of experiencing the broadening of its scope in the newly formed 'Welfare State'. As the role of the government expanded, there obviously were occasions when the government did fell short of the extremely high levels of standards of managing its business, as set in the Constitution of India, and expectations in general from the prominent individuals managing the government, who till the other day were the front rank freedom fighters. With an independent and fearless judiciary established by the Constitution of India, such gaps between high expectations and low performance were brought before the concerned judicial forum for proper redressal.

Since independence, and especially after the adoption of the Constitution of India on 26 November 1949, the courts did not shy away from playing the role of an unbiased and neutral observer, without getting overly and proactively involved, in deciding whatever matters were brought before them on the basis of the well-established principles of law, most of them having been duly incorporated into the relevant statutes, and in choosing strict legality as the guiding light and in not pronouncing judgements based on sheer whims and fancies. But, with the passage of time as the society was evolving and the aspirations of the people were changing, it was found on a couple of occasions that the judicial pronouncements were not, in real sense, helping the people of the country, though application of legal principles strictly had been the sole criterion while pronouncing those decisions.

A case in point is that related to sovereign immunity and loss of gold from a police station, which we will discuss a little later in this chapter. The judiciary responded well to the changing role of the government and expectations from it in later judgements as the bar for judging the government was raised higher and higher, with emphasis on fundamental rights of the citizens gaining importance increasingly. The ever expanding interpretation of the fundamental rights truly brought under its ambit numerous privileges for the people of India, including foreigners, who wished to do business in India, and at the same time made the job of the government markedly difficult and onerous. The trend continues.

Post emergency in mid-1970s, when the country had gone through the worse suppression of rights and privileges, the Supreme Court rose to the occasion and worked proactively to protect the rights of the people of India with unforeseen zeal and enthusiasm. It gave rise to the PIL in the country, and the doors of the courts, especially the higher courts (high courts and the Supreme Court), were opened to the people in a manner never experienced before. Interpretations of the relevant articles of the Constitution providing for the working of the higher courts in the country were reinterpreted to give them powers, including the power to take suo motu action if needed, in cases of administrative remiss and amiss. It is debatable whether these powers were already with the higher courts, which had never been used or had been rarely used in smallest of the measures and with great caution, or these powers were the result of encroaching into the till then widely accepted powers of the legislature and executive.

This debate among jurists technically remains inconclusive; however, practically it is well established that the role of the higher courts in India saw a sea change in the late 1970s, and the next two decades—1980s and 1990s—saw pathbreaking decisions related to human rights, environment, child labour, condition of prisoners, historical monuments, etc. 'Judicial activism', the phrase used to describe the new role of the higher judiciary, became the key phrase and was very often used not only in legal discussions, but normal and casual discussions at the coffee table and the dinner table. This wave of judicial activism slowly but surely had its impact on the infrastructure projects in the country. Before moving on to the role of judiciary in infrastructure projects, let us go briefly through the case about sovereign immunity and stolen gold.

CASE STUDY

Loss of Gold from Police Station Case[42]

It so happened that on 20 September 1947, about a month after India gained independence on 15 August 1947, one Ralia Ram who used to deal in bullion and other goods at Amritsar arrived at Meerut by the Frontier Mail. He was carrying with him gold, silver and other goods. On suspicion that he was carrying stolen goods, the police took him into custody and confiscated substantial quantity of gold and silver which were kept in the vault at the police station. The head constable, about a month later, fled away to Pakistan with the gold and silver. Ralia Ram was able to prove that he was the rightful owner of the precious metals but by that time the goods were not available in police custody.

He demanded his goods back, and in case the goods being unavailable with the police, the price of the goods as on that date. It was not very difficult because the weight of gold and silver which had been taken into custody from Ralia Ram was noted down and was in the police records. As the goods were not available, the police could have very well settled the account by paying the equivalent amount of money as on that date; however, the police stated that it was performing a sovereign function and hence it was not liable to pay anything to Ralia Ram. It was shocking for him as he could have never imagined that gold and silver confiscated from him by the police would never be returned to him, though he was the rightful owner and was in lawful possession in Meerut.

He moved to the court for recovery of equivalent amount of money or the precious metals and the trial court decided in his favour on the basis of two issues framed. First, the police personnel were negligent and, second, whether he should be compensated. The trial court held that the police were negligent and thus must compensate. The state of Uttar Pradesh appealed

---

[42] *Kasturilal Ralia Ram Jain v. The State Of Uttar Pradesh*, Supreme Court of India, 29 September 1964, Bench: P. B. Gajendragadkar (CJ), K. N. Wanchoo, M. Hidayatullah, Raghubar Dayal, J. R. Mudholkar, JJ.; 1965 AIR 1039, 1965 SCR (1) 375.

in the high court, which decided that the police were not negligent and hence there was no question of compensation. The high court went a step further and observed that even if the police were negligent, there could not be a money decree against the state of Uttar Pradesh for negligence of the police as it were performing sovereign functions. Challenging this decision, an appeal was filed in the Supreme Court of India. After hearing the parties in detail, the Supreme Court concluded that the Uttar Pradesh police was definitely negligent in handling the goods confiscated from Ralia Ram and observed:

> Thus considered, there can be no escape from the conclusion that the police officers were negligent in dealing with Ralia Ram's property after it was seized from him. Not only was the property not kept in safe custody in the treasury, but the manner in which it was dealt with at the Malkhana shows gross negligence on the part of the police officers.[43]

Ironically, the Supreme Court bench of five judges did not agree for a money decree, despite proven negligence on the part of the state police. Citing numerous cases and well-established legal principles, most of them being borrowed from the British law, the court did not compensate Ralia Ram, however, expressed its disbelief on the state of affairs because of the legal position and technicalities, simply put the blame on the legislature and lamented in the following words:

> In dealing with the present appeal, we have ourselves been disturbed by the thought that a citizen whose property was seized by process of law, has to be told when he seeks a remedy in a court of law on the ground that his property has not been returned to him, that he can make no claim against the State. That, we think, is not a very satisfactory position in law. The remedy to cure this position, however, lies in the bands of the Legislature.[44]

It surely was a most unsatisfactory and unconvincing decision which truly brought forth the limitations within which the Supreme Court bench was making the decision rather than

---

[43] Ibid.
[44] Ibid.

exercising wide discretion it is empowered with by the Constitution of India. Most unfortunate!

The trend of judicial pronouncements since then, luckily for the citizens of India, has changed to make the State answerable and also compensate for the negligence of people acting as agents of the State.

CASE STUDY

Flemingo Duty-Free Shop v. Union of India (UOI), Bombay High Court, 2008[45]

Mumbai's airport has been a very busy airport in India for a very long time, and with the increase in number of flights and passengers, the international airport needed immediate upgradation at the turn of the century. Also, the aspirations of Indian passengers were high and with more exposure due to foreign travel, they were more demanding as compared to the earlier times. As we have discussed in earlier chapters that infusion of money and other resources for the government had not been possible due to other more demanding sectors, hence, PPP was considered to be the best method to get the purpose served. With this final goal in mind, a JV company named MIAL was registered under the Companies Act, 1956.

It was a consortium of a few Indian and foreign companies, following the then norms of foreign investment and sharing. The MIAL was responsible for almost everything related to the airport, especially its management. It operated under the control of the government and the AAI. The management of

---

[45] (1) *Flemingo Duty-Free Shop Private Limited*; (2) *Vivek S. Bhatt v.* (1) *Union of India*; (2) *Airports Authority of India*; (3) *Mumbai International Airports Private Limited*; (4) *Itdc Aldeasa India Private Limited*; (5) *DFS Venture Singapore (Pte) Limited*; (6) *DFS India Private Limited*; Bombay High Court; 05 Jun 2008; Bench: D. K. Deshmukh and N. D. Deshpande, JJ.; Citations: 2008 (4) AllMR 663, 2008 INDLAW MUM 228.

the international airport at Mumbai, the Chhatrapati Shivaji International Airport (CSIA), was transferred by the AAI to MIAL for 30 years, renewable for another 30 years, through an agreement called the Operation, Management and Development Agreement (OMDA) in 2006. The MIAL planned for duty-free shops at the airport and for this purpose called for expression of interest (EOI). Flemingo, an Indian company, submitted its EOI along with its Irish JV partner Aer Rianta International.

Flemingo was invited by the MIAL to make a presentation and also to furnish details about its business. Thereafter, Flemingo did not hear anything from the MIAL about its participation in the process of shortlisting. It was not informed anything about the tender documents; however, it got to know that some other participants had been issued the RfP. Flemingo filed a writ petition in the Bombay High Court challenging the procedure followed by the MIAL and not issuing it the RfP. After a little bit of roller-coaster ride in legal forums, including the Supreme Court on legal technicality and other writ petitions challenging the award of contract to other participants, the Bombay High Court finally heard the matter in 2008.

The MIAL defended its position by stating that Flemingo was not shortlisted and hence was not issued RfP. Moreover, the MIAL is not 'State' as defined in Article 12 of the Constitution of India and, therefore, no writ petition lies against it. Article 12 of the Constitution of India is as follows:

> In this Part, unless the context otherwise requires, 'the State' includes the Government and Parliament of India and the Government and the Legislature of each of the States and all local or other authorities within the territory of India or under the control of the Government of India.

This is in Part III of the Constitution, which includes the fundamental rights. A writ petition for protection of fundamental rights can be filed in the Supreme Court under Article 32, and in the high courts under Article 226 for fundamental rights and other rights also. However, this has to be directed against the State only.

The pertinent question to be answered in the instant case was whether the MIAL was covered under the definition of the State or not. In case, the MIAL was held to be a private entity, there would have been no reason for filing a writ petition, as private entities are not covered under Part I of the Constitution and are not legally bound to protect different fundamental rights, the most important being the right to equality and the right to be treated fairly. In brief, a private party can act in any manner it likes, however, within the legal framework, but is not to worry about giving equal and fair opportunity to everyone with whom it does its business. The State entities do not have the freedom to do so.

They have to take every care to be just, fair, reasonable and provide equal opportunity to all concerned. The primary reason is that the State cannot act arbitrarily and must exercise discretion in a manner which is reasonable and relevant in any given context. Flemingo's counsel argued that 26 per cent of shareholding in the MIAL was held by the AAI, and the MIAL was given the power to perform those functions of the AAI which were mentioned in the lease. There was also an agreement between the MIAL and the GoI known as the State Support Agreement (SSA) to provide all governmental services to the MIAL. It is understood that in a JV where the government has 50 per cent or more share, it is deemed to be a government company, that is, State under Article 12.

In case this share reduces to less than 50 per cent, it would be erroneous to call that company a purely private company. It remains a PPP and hence should be dealt like the State. And, as the MIAL was given all the powers of the AAI by OMDA, the MIAL was performing functions, which included the functions performed by State, as the AAI is undoubtedly State. The lease between the MIAL and the AAI was mainly 'in the public interest or in the interest of better management of airports' according to the AAI Act, 1994, as amended in 2003. The lessee was expected and authorized to carry out the functions of the lessor, the AAI, and hence, is surely an instrumentality or agency of the State, and must be covered by Article 12.

While inviting bids, the MIAL was supposed to mention clearly the criteria for selection and due process must have been followed. Instead, it had chosen to whimsically reject the participation of Flemingo without assigning any reason. An instrumentality of State cannot conduct itself in this manner. Legal certainty was required with transparency in the functioning of the MIAL, and the bidding process should have been without any opacity. Arbitrary action by the MIAL resulted in prejudice to Flemingo and made the selection process unfair and against public interest. It was also argued that even if the MIAL was not held to be State, still the high court could issue writ against it under Article 226 for violation of legal right. This was a little far-fetched as any writ is not issued against an entity which is not State.

Surprisingly, the MIAL's argument was based on the fact that it was a purely private company and incorporated for making profits. The relationship of the MIAL with any shop would have been simply contractual and for such matters, no writ against a private party would be maintainable. Also, the MIAL declined that there was any obligation for it to give any reasons for not shortlisting or shortlisting any participant for the bidding process. This, frankly speaking, does not make any sense in a PPP, for the simple reason that a PPP is not a purely private entity and is conceptually an amalgamation of private and public enterprise.

There cannot be any PPP without the participation of a public entity, and the only question to be answered is as to what can be the criteria to decide whether the created PPP entity is of private or public nature. One thing is quite obvious: the PPP cannot just absolve itself of all public duties and get rid of public interest from its charter of responsibilities. It would be a mockery of the entire exercise of bringing together the public and private sector together if the public perspective can very conveniently be erased from the large canvas of nation building and doing something purposeful for the public. The Supreme Court did not agree with the stand taken by the MIAL that it was merely a private entity and existed only for making profits.

The court held that the purpose of creation of the MIAL was fundamentally for public interest and, hence, the MIAL should have conducted itself at least with some semblance of a public entity, if not getting into the shoes of the State as such. In no case, the MIAL could have worked as a purely private company and avoided taking care of the fundamental rights of the participants to the selection process for award of a contract for the duty-free shop. A bald decision, without any reasons, could not be expected from the MIAL. In the instant case, forget about the reasons, the MIAL did not even inform Flemingo that its EOI had been rejected and that it did not qualify for the next stage of the bidding process. Finally, the Bombay High Court set aside the contract awarded to another participant and ordered for fresh advertisements and selection according to provisions of law applicable to public bodies. The court held:

> We, thus, find that the Respondent No. 3 is in truth and substance is an instrumentality of the State and is, therefore, bound by Part-III of the Constitution.[46]

All sort of legal technicalities were used to fail Flemingo's petition, including the one that the Irish partner was not made a party to the petition, and that Flemingo should not have even submitted its EOI if it was not satisfied and convinced with the process, or rather lack of it, mentioned in the advertisement and that submission of EOI stopped Flemingo from objecting later on. Nothing was accepted by the Bombay High Court and, in very brief, the court held that a JV formed under a PPP, with substantial powers of a public body, can never be a pure private entity.

---

[46] Ibid.

JUDICIAL ACTIVISM

There has been a streak of independence and a sort of rebellion in the manner of judicial pronouncements since the formation of the Supreme Court in 1950, as was very evident with the newly found independence and sovereign powers, but the heavy burden of the former British rule coupled with deep infusion of inferiority complex, intentionally done by the English rule for more than two centuries, did not permit the Indian judiciary to really shed the cloak of colonialism so easily. It took a while. Only when the country was being transformed towards a more egalitarian and socialistic set-up in the early 1970s with nationalization of banks, abolition of privy purses and the call in the country for alleviation of poverty, though political class deep inside wanted to let the people of India poor and illiterate forever as it suited their political plans, the judiciary felt the unease and made up its mind to face the political masters.

That was the time when the landmark judgement—Kesavananda Bharati[47]—was pronounced establishing the basic structure doctrine forever. It was that time when the judiciary invalidated the law made by the legislative body by amendments on the grounds of changing the basic structure of the Constitution of India. Since then, judicial activism has been in vogue in the system; however, it became more visible and effective in late 1970s. Judicial review of administrative actions has become routine. Interpretation of 'state' has been widened and 'locus standi' has received almost a new meaning in case of PIL.

---

[47] *Kesavananda Bharati Sripadagalvaru and Ors. v. State of Kerala and Anr.*, (1973) 4 SCC 225.

CASE STUDY

Pathan Mohammed v. State of Gujarat, Supreme Court of India, 2013[48]

This was a PIL filed in the Gujarat High Court by Pathan Mohammed against allocation of land to Gujarat International Finance Tec-City (GIFT) based on the adverse report of Comptroller and Auditor General of India (CAG). The PIL was dismissed and, hence, Pathan Mohammed appealed in the Supreme Court. At the turn of the century when economic liberalization had settled a bit, and investors and entrepreneurs were restless to have something big, just like what they had witnessed and experienced abroad, the state of Gujarat took the initiative of creating a special area which would provide all the necessary things for businesses at one place along with simple rules and regulations and ease of procedure.

Basically, the idea was to have something on the lines of international finance centres like Shinjuku in Tokyo, Lujiazui in Shanghai, La Défense in Paris, London Docklands, Dubai International Financial Centre (DIFC) in Dubai, etc., all of which typically have flexibility of functioning, administrative machinery, rules and regulations, attractive exemptions for businesses and almost everything conceivable to do business in an easy manner leading to convenience and profits. This has been experienced as a win-win situation for businesses and society where everything needed for doing business easily—physical and tangible things, licences and approvals, government support, least intervention of judicial process and, above all, proper infrastructure —is arranged and ensured at one place. Having everything at one place gives tremendous confidence to businesses, and investors are willing to take a chance by investing even in risky propositions as there is faith and trust in the government's intentions. So creating an international financial centre was definitely considered to be a giant leap for attracting investments.

---

[48] *Pathan Mohammed Suleman Rehmatkhan v. State of Gujarat and others;* Supreme Court of India; 22 November 2013; Bench: K. S. Radhakrishnan, A. K. Sikri, JJ.; Reported in 2013 Indlaw SC 771; JT 2014 (1) SC 303; 2013(14) SCALE 385; S.L.P. (C) No. 32507 of 2013.

The plan was approved by the state government; however, lack of resources with the state, as usually is the case always with any state, compelled the state to go with the PPP model, and it was decided to secure private funding for the GIFT city. There were many takers and the IL&FS took the lead in making the commitment at the right time for forming a JV with the state government. Thus, GIFT city was incorporated as a company with a 50–50 partnership between the IL&FS and the state of Gujarat. Huge tracts of land were allotted by the state government to the GIFT city. The GoI approved the GIFT city under the Special Economic Zones Act, 2005.

Money was made available to create the necessary infrastructure in the GIFT city and construction work started in full swing. In its report of 2013, the CAG made certain remarks about the process of allocation of land and issues which had emerged after the performance audit. It was categorically mentioned that the Gujarat government did not comply with all the necessary statutory and regulatory requirements, and no proper policy was followed in allocation of land to the GIFT city. It was also stated that a huge chunk of state revenue had got blocked because of this project and there was no mechanism for proper review and monitoring. The concluding portion of the CAG report mentioned:

> The performance audit revealed a number of system and compliance deficiencies. Government did not adopt a uniform policy in alienation and allotment of land. Delay in finalisation of valuation also resulted in blocking up of revenue of the Government. There was no mechanism for review and revision of incorrect orders issued by the subordinate officers to safeguard Government revenue. No proper monitoring system exists in the Department to ascertain and vacate encroachment cases.

These were very serious allegations. The Gujarat High Court was of the opinion that there had been inordinate delay in filing the PIL; however, as these issues were of public interest, the court heard the matter on merits and decided that these were policy decisions based on the policy objectives of the state government, and that the CAG had no authority to question the policy decisions. The petition was dismissed, which prompted the petitioner to file a special leave petition (SLP) in the Supreme Court. After discussing the immense importance of CAG in the Indian system of parliamentary control, the Supreme Court observed that, however, it was the government which was directly responsible for the functioning of the administration and also accountable to the people. In such a situation, it was neither possible nor desirable to have every decision made by the government scrutinized minutely.

Moreover, this scrutiny is always done after the time has passed for making the decision and implementing it. Thus, for all practical purposes it was like a post-mortem of the democratically elected governments, which make decisions in good faith. It is quite a possibility that some of the decisions may prove wrong in the long run, but that does not make the decision made by the government intentional wrongdoing. It was simply a matter of chance that some decisions may not prove to be beneficial, neither to the people of the area, nor the private entity joining hands with the government. After going through all the documents of the project, the Supreme Court agreed with the high court that it could not be said that the government acted against public interest.

On another issue mentioned in the CAG report that the government had authorized the GIFT city to mortgage or lease the land, despite the ownership being with the government, there was a very strong opinion that such a provision in the CA was without any doubt against the basic principles of ownership and grant of a lease. It is definitely baffling that how could a lessee mortgage portion of the land without taking formal and express approval from the lessor. It was quite right for the CAG to point out this anomaly; however, the Supreme Court did not pay much attention and rejected CAG's objection on the one and only ground that all those decisions made were policy decisions, and it was for the government of the day to make those decisions and that judiciary should not interfere with policy decisions.

There is always a very thin dividing line between pure policy decisions and policy decisions which have practical implications and thereby cannot always be said to be beyond the purview of judiciary. Something analogous is like a question of fact or question of law, and whenever these two are intertwined, it itself is concerned to be a question of law rather than a question of fact as is well known to practitioners of law in appellate courts. For certain matters and in some courts, only questions of law can be raised, as facts are supposed to be well established at the trial court itself.

A policy decision made by the legislature and thereafter implemented by the executive, which practically is the legislature and executive rolled into one in most of the democratic countries with a party or coalition controlling the majority of seats in the legislative body, can by itself not shut the doors of judicial review. The Supreme Court's view to distance itself from these decisions, which may be called policy decisions but truly have great impact on the ground, is perplexing. Chastising the CAG for doing its duty and pointing out fingers at hollow spaces, without going into the merits of each of the points highlighted in the report, the Supreme Court missed a very good opportunity to strengthen the functioning of the CAG and giving the right signal to the business fraternity and the government that procedural law is as important as substantive law, if not more.

This should have been highlighted and given due importance for something happening in the state of Gujarat, the place where Gandhi, the Father of the Nation, was born and had always preached and practised that means were more important than the end. It is surely praiseworthy to have a free zone business which can be conducted easily and private enterprise is attracted to such land of opportunities; however, proper procedural aspects have to be taken care of and, more so, when something of such scale and magnitude is being done for the very first time. It helps to be cautious and being cautious pays in the long run.

COLLAPSE OF THE IL&FS

As discussed in the previous chapter, the IL&FS collapsed in 2018 and the future of the GIFT city came under dark clouds.[49] As the legal entity, GIFT City Co. Ltd was the 50–50 JV between the IL&FS and the Gujarat Urban Development Corporation (GUDC), a distinct legal entity owned by the state of Gujarat, with funding being primarily provided by the IL&FS, heavy turbulence was faced by the project leading to the Gujarat government stating that it will itself somehow fund the project and buy out the share of the IL&FS.[50] It may be a strong possibility as there are a large number of private investors looking for business opportunity in the GIFT city and thus making huge profits in the times to come; however, there are surely certain doubts about the manner in which the project took off from the ground in the initial phase, especially at the stage of getting approvals.

Was due diligence not done at that time? It is the same question which was asked by CAG in its report but was brushed aside in court proceedings. The deal between the government of Gujarat and the IL&FS at that time had also been in dispute due to heavy consultancy fee charged by the IL&FS for setting up the project, which according to many observers got them the initial amount they had invested back very soon. Also, IL&FS-appointed consultants were paid huge sums of money as consultancy fee.[51] In brief, it appears that the state of Gujarat was excessively milked by IL&FS top brass.

---

[49] Maulik Pathak, 'GIFT City's Future Hangs in Balance,' *The Times of India*, 12 March 2019. Available at https://timesofindia.indiatimes.com/city/ahmedabad/gift citys-future-hangs-in-balance/articleshow/68365937.cms (accessed on 25 April 2019).

[50] Dev Chatterjee, 'Gujarat Will Buy Crisis-Hit IL&FS Stake in GIFT City, Says CM Vijay Rupani,' *Business Standard*, 27 November 2019. Available at https://www.business-standard.com/article/companies/gujarat-will-buy-crisis-hit-il-fs-stake-in-gift-city-says-cm-vijay-rupani-118112600980_1.html (accessed on 25 April 2019).

[51] Sucheta Dalal, 'Is GIFT City Gujarat's Gift to IL&FS through One-Sided Deals?' *Money Life*, 9 August 2018. Available at https://www.moneylife.in/article/is-gift-city-gujarats-gift-to-ilfs-through-one-sided-deals/54961.html (accessed on 25 April 2019).

WRIT JURISDICTION OF THE SUPREME COURT AND THE HIGH COURTS

There are five types of writs which can be filed in the high courts and the Supreme Court. These are habeas corpus, certiorari, prohibition, mandamus and quo warranto. The primary purpose of these writs is to have a judicial check on the discretionary power of the administrative authorities. India is committed to 'rule of law' which means that ultimately what matters is the law and not any individual or any official position. It is also said that rule of law, in other words, means 'be you ever so high, the law is above you'. To ensure that rule of law prevails, the courts are equipped with certain powers of writ jurisdiction by the Constitution of India. The most important provisions in the Constitution for this purpose are Articles 32 and 226. Article 32, also called the Right to Constitutional Remedies, reads as follows:

> 32. Remedies for enforcement of rights conferred by this Part.
>
> (1) The right to move the Supreme Court by appropriate proceedings for the enforcement of the rights conferred by this Part is guaranteed.
>
> (2) The Supreme Court shall have power to issue directions or orders or writs, including writs in the nature of *habeas* cor*pus*, *mandamus*, prohibition, *quo warranto* and *certiorari*, whichever may be appropriate, for the enforcement of any of the rights conferred by this Part.

Article 32, itself, is a fundamental right and is often said to be the 'heart and soul' of the Constitution of India. There is no practical purpose of guaranteeing fundamental rights if the violation of those rights cannot be protected by a legal remedy, and that's precisely the reason why Article 32 provides these legal remedies, as a fundamental right itself, against the mighty State. This legal remedy is to be used only in cases when the other statutory remedies—alternative remedies—have been exhausted or are simply not available. Article 226 is somewhat similar and provides these powers to the high courts, along with a little bit more scope for intervention in cases of violation of any legal right. It reads as follows:

> 226. Power of High Courts to issue certain writs.
>
> (1) Notwithstanding anything in Article 32, every High Court shall have power, throughout the territories in relation to which it exercises jurisdiction, to issue to any person or authority, including in appropriate cases, any Government, within those territories directions, orders or writs, including writs in the nature of *habeas corpus, mandamus*, prohibition, *quo warranto* and *certiorari*, or any of them, for the enforcement of any of the rights conferred by Part III and for any other purpose.

The same condition applies as in Article 32. There should not be any other statutory alternative remedy, and in case there is a remedy available, it should have been exhausted by the petitioner before moving the high court. There can be rare exceptions when the high courts may exercise discretion to entertain any petition even when the alternative remedy has not been exhausted; however, this can only be in extreme conditions when certain other exigencies make it compelling for the high courts to intervene and take up the matter for hearing. These provisions and practices have been in vogue for a very long time and have been sharpened by numerous decisions of the high courts and the Supreme Court so as to prepare broad guidelines for petitioners, though the ultimate power of discretion still remains with the bench hearing a matter on a particular date. There can be extraordinary circumstances usually adversely impacting public interest which force the judiciary to intercede.

Part III of the Constitution deals with fundamental rights. One of the important differences between Articles 32 and 226 is that the former is limited only to the rights conferred by Part III of the Constitution, as the words used in Article 32(2) are '...for the enforcement of any of the rights conferred by this Part', whereas the latter can be used for other rights also as the words used in Article 226(1) are '...for the enforcement of any of the rights conferred by Part III and for any other purpose'. The words 'for any other purpose' are extremely important in giving a much larger scope to the high courts in issuing writs for violation of rights not necessarily fundamental in nature. This is one article which gives the opportunity to almost every aggrieved party to move the high court against the mighty State and is definitely used very often in all the high courts of the country.

As these writs are prerogative in nature—discretion of the judges, as was the case in England when the writs were issued by the King—their efficacy lies in the manner in which the judges take up the case. With the growth of administrative law, the judiciary in India has expanded the scope of the writs, for all practical purposes and with the advent of PIL, the writs have found new usage, sometimes making the otherwise optional decisions mandatory for the government. The nature of the writ of mandamus has been expanded like anything in the last four decades or so, very often leaving the government with hardly any choice of judgement.

The writ of mandamus, as the name suggests (mandamus is a Latin word meaning 'we command'), is an order from the superior court to any inferior court, or the government, or any public authority to do something, or not to do something, according to the law of the land. The important issue in this writ is that there is a certain duty assigned to that body to do, or not to do, something and the superior courts commands it to perform it. This writ ensures that the public bodies perform within their legally determined periphery and never to transgress it. Also, it is important that they should not remain inactive and complacent and never go anywhere near the periphery, that is, choose not to do anything. It is one of the most commonly used writs for getting relief in infrastructure PPP projects.

The writ of certiorari is issued by superior courts against lower courts or quasi-judicial bodies. It is mainly a direction by the higher courts to lower courts to send the proceedings of a case for judicial scrutiny to ensure the legality of orders. Certiorari is a Latin word meaning 'to certify'. If the decisions made by the lower court do not pass the test of legal scrutiny, they are quashed by the higher courts, and the case is usually remanded back to the lower court with directions to be followed while deciding it afresh. Thus, this writ gives the adjudicating body to correct itself by aligning with the higher courts' directions. Principles of natural justice play an important role as one of the most prevalent test for clearing the bar in higher courts.

The writ of 'prohibition' is to prevent a judicial or quasi-judicial body from transgressing its jurisdiction, or hearing and deciding matters for which they have no jurisdiction at all. The word prohibition means to order a lower court to stop from proceeding further. In common parlance, it is also called a 'stay order' and is often sought for any court or other quasi-judicial proceedings which are ongoing, and the presiding officer continues to proceed with the matter despite not having the jurisdiction, and after dismissing the objections raised by the affected party not to exercise the non-existent jurisdiction. This is one way of the superior courts to stop the inferior courts from conducting themselves arbitrarily. This writ is very effective to control irresponsible and reckless judicial and quasi-judicial officers.

The purpose of certiorari and prohibition is the same—preventing miscarriage of justice; however, in the former the writ is issued after the order has been passed by the lower court, whereas in the latter the stay is granted during the pendency of case in the lower court.

The writ of quo warranto is used to stop a person from holding a public office he might have usurped. Quo warranto literally means 'by what authority'. Thus, if a person somehow manages to be in an administrative position to which he is not entitled to, he may possibly cause substantial damage by issuing orders and making decisions detrimental to public interest. Also, it shall be a mockery of the administrative machinery where someone is acting without authority and there is no one to check him or her. The writ is very useful and effective in case there is forceful taking over of certain official position, or a person takes advantage of prevailing confusion and acts on his own wrongful assumptions of having the authority to act upon. A few practical examples can be a person acting and issuing orders even after retirement or transfer.

The writ of habeas corpus is seldom used in commercial matters. It is the writ issued by higher courts to ensure the production of a person in the court, who has been detained by the State or any private person. It is one of the exceptional writs which can be issued against a private person also. Literally, habeas corpus means to have the body. Thus, the legal person against whom the writ is issued has to produce the detained person in the court and if the detention is not according to the law of the land, he shall be released by the court. In India, the law says—in Article 21 of the Constitution—that 'no person shall be deprived of his life or personal liberty except according to the procedure established by law'.

This is one of the most important fundamental rights and the writ of habeas corpus finds its use usually against controversial detentions by the State; however, in infrastructure projects there can sometimes be so much enmity between competing contractors that the unscrupulous business persons may stoop down to illegally detaining—which includes unlawful restraining one's liberty—either the competitor or his workers. Thankfully, these incidents are rare, but unfortunately they do happen and the aggrieved party gets compelled to move to the high court or the Supreme Court to get the detained persons released safely and timely. The writ can obviously not be filed by the detained person; it has to be filed by someone close to him or an interested person. The courts can take up the matter suo motu also if they get the information about someone's illegal detention.

KEY TAKEAWAYS

- *Access to courts:* The courts in India—right up to the Supreme Court—are accessible to everyone, and with the rise in population and growing awareness about legal rights, there has been an explosion of litigation. The situation in the country is very different from that at the time of independence as far as legal awareness and legal literacy are concerned. The class divide has been bridged to a large extent due to the rising middle class and expansion of education. The higher courts—the high courts and the Supreme Court—have opened their doors for everyone through the PIL movement and, hence, the exclusive access to courts for the rich and well connected only has been diluted considerably.

- *Delay in judicial proceedings:* Tremendous increase in the social welfare legislation has resulted in heavy filing of cases for seeking legal remedy for the deprived sections of society. The courts have also started taking up various causes related to social justice, environment degradation, cleansing of the political system and various other issues in public interest. Provisions of various appeals in different statutes and procedural rigmarole often lead to delay in judicial proceedings. The most troublesome feature of the Indian judicial system is the inordinate delay due to so many reasons, and despite many judicial reforms, the proceedings have not yet been expedited to the desired levels. Business executives should keep this in mind while formulating their business strategy.

- *Wise and wide discretion:* The judges in the higher courts have been given discretionary power—both wise and wide—which they are expected to exercise with due caution and utmost responsibility. Sometimes, the persona of a judge may be at variance with his real self, thus creating the problem of serious conflicts with oneself in exercising discretion. When judges exhibit moral flexibility in the application of the same legal principle in different manners in two or more sets of facts, uncontrollable problems arise for the parties and others in the country, as the judgements have the power of precedence. More and more objectivity is desirable with very little subjectivity to be left at the discretion of the judge. But even infinitesimally small discretion can be damaging if exercised in a whimsical manner.

Chapter 7
POLITICAL WILL AND INTENTION

It is without any doubt the duty of the government to provide proper infrastructure to the people in any country; however, the reasons for doing so may vary from country to country and even within a country like India from state to state. The basic understanding that good infrastructure does help in overall growth and development of economy is not at all in dispute. That is precisely why, in the long run, infrastructure must be maintained and new additions should be done at regular intervals. The primary motive of the powers in a jurisdiction making suitable decisions is, surprisingly, not the same. In a monarchy, with a benevolent monarch in power, the resources of the nation are directed towards nation building leading to increasing happiness of the people.

On the other hand, with autocratic governments in power, the national resources are shamelessly used for the benefit of the autocrat, without bothering about the dismal state of living of the ordinary masses. Democracies like India choose their own fate in the form of elected leaders, who may be kicked out of power if they do not show results within a reasonable period of time, and if they are not able to keep the people happy. Democratic compulsions for elected leaders, howsoever good-intentioned and visionary they may be, sometimes do not let them make the necessary hard decisions, which are good in the long run, but at any particular moment appear to be extremely harsh, unnecessary and totally avoidable.

Building infrastructure is a long-term endeavour and requires consistent and unbroken train of thoughts, policies and execution. This is always not possible due to a variety of reasons. Globally, most of the countries, except those which are sitting on a pile of cash, and their governments are the main funding institutions, infrastructure development is heavily dependent on PPPs. It becomes the most obvious method of creating infrastructure. Large economies, with substantial presence of private enterprise, use the PPP model to make the optimal use of available resources, but economies heavily dependent on the government and, thus, dependent on public investment with almost absence of private enterprise, do not incline towards the PPP model. Life may appear to be simpler in terms of contractual obligations, accounting and legal wrangles in these jurisdictions; however, in these places, infrastructure development usually lacks the variety of bright colours and vibrancy, that is, a mix of many styles and features in the final result.

Typically, private enterprise brings with it variation, greater imagination and in general pushing the perception frontier to new vistas. PPPs bring in the best of private zeal and enthusiasm, along with the greater sense of risk management by the government. The role of the governments, more so in democratic countries, is of ensuring accountability of the private entity to the public, and not only to the leader of the government. The elected governments are themselves answerable to the public and, hence, despite the usual hue and cry in PPP projects about misappropriation of funds and graft, varying from very small and insignificant proportions to very high and obscene levels, there is definitely an effective control, howsoever subtle it may be, of the public over the PPP projects.

Political will and intention are necessary for making speedy decisions and earmarking huge chunks of money for infrastructure projects. What sort of projects will be given priority is also a very important decision to be made by the political leadership as it will have long-lasting impact on the people of the country in the form of infrastructure which will be created for generations. For instance, in certain countries where road construction has been given priority over creating a network of railways, one can see in the long run a large network of highways along with the need to have cars and other automobiles, rather than railway wagons and engines, which itself gives a different direction to the economy, that is, to automobiles and related industries.

It will also have an impact on the ancillary units which develop along with the main factories to make automobiles. Banks and financial institutions making loans easily available for automobiles give a new dimension to the economy and there are chances of insurance business also getting a shot in the arm as more roads with more automobiles have higher chance of resulting in higher number of accidents. Thus, one decision by the political leadership, which shows the intention and the will, can have an effect on several sectors of economy and for generations. These decisions, therefore, provide a bearing to the political thought process.

COMPULSIONS OF COALITION POLITICS

The will and intention of political party A and political party B may be very different, as guided by their political ideology and philosophy. With periodic elections—every five years in India for the central government—there is always the risk of a shift in the will and intention of the government if the ruling party is not re-elected. In case the mood of the country is to change the party in power and bring the other party to power, there is clarity about the path to be followed by the party which comes to power as usually it is clearly, at least broadly, laid down in the party manifesto made public during the election. So it can be said that broadly the contours of policy formulation and execution are known to the people and based on these promises choices are made for casting the ballot.

The problem becomes extremely complex, and at times ugly, when one single party is not able to get sufficient number of seats and is dependent on either independent legislators or some small political parties for supporting one of the largest parties to form the government. Countries with two-party system—such as the USA and the UK—do not face this problem, but India has often encountered this problem with numerous political parties at the central and state levels. Coalition governments are bound to follow the coalition dharma, as mentioned by several political commentators, writers, journalists and most importantly the prime minister of the country himself.

In 2008, the UPA government at the centre, headed by Dr Manmohan Singh as the prime minister, faced serious issues about conflicting intentions and will of coalition partners making it extremely difficult, almost impossible, to make decisions rationally and independently. A large number of infrastructure projects in the country, including the ambitious Golden Quadrilateral project connecting the four metropolitan cities of India and launched in 2001 by the NDA government, got slowed down because of irreconcilable differences between the coalition partners. The country was facing 'policy paralysis', a phrase which became very popular during that period of time to convey the helplessness of the government in making decisions.

The situation gave the chance to the opposition leader, L. K. Advani, to make the comment that Dr Manmohan Singh was *nikamma* (good-for-nothing) prime minister. In response to the trust vote motion because of the nuclear liability issues, Dr Singh replied in the Parliament and emphasized on the fact that he was not a worthless prime minister and he had been doing his best for the country within the given constraints of coalition politics and taking the supporting parties along. He made it very clear in his reply that in a coalition government it was not possible for the majority party to make decisions on its own which have to be in consultation with the coalition partners and these were in fact the obstacles in a speedy and effective decision-making.

He, inter alia, said:

> This I believe is a measure of the respect that the world at large has for India, its people and their capabilities and our prospects to emerge as a major engine of growth for the world economy. I have often said that today there are no international constraints on India's development. The world marvels at our ability to seek our social and economic salvation in the framework of a functioning democracy committed to the rule of law and respect for fundamental human freedoms. The world wants India to succeed. The obstacles we face are at home, particularly in our processes of domestic governance.[52]

What he said had, and still has, great relevance in international relations, international trade, foreign investment, transnational business and the confidence the world has in India. His words, '…the world wants India to succeed…' have special significance. The world cannot afford India to fail and the primary reason is that India is a huge democratic

---

[52] *The Times of India*, 'Advani Called Me *Nikamma* PM: Manmohan,' 22 July 2008. Available at http://timesofindia.indiatimes.com/articleshow/3265909.cms (accessed on 25 April 2019).

country with a population of more than 1.3 billion, and the world shudders even at the thought of the possibility of India not channelizing the energy of its people in the positive direction. If the country fails, this humongous energy will obviously get directed towards negativity damaging the humanity in all sort of unacceptable ways.

There can be serious disruption in global peace and security. To prevent any such thing, it is in the world's interest that India succeeds. In addition, stability and positivism will lead to business-friendly environment, giving wonderful opportunity to the developed world to invest its surplus cash reserves for superior ROI. Prosperous India will create better market for selling goods and services of the multinational companies, which again is in the interest of the developed world as most of the highly successful companies are incorporated in the first-world countries.

THE BIG DIG, BOSTON

Boston has been one of the oldest cities in the USA and had played an important role in the American Revolution. The city is famous, among other things, for the Boston Tea Party, a political and commercial protest against imposition of tax for selling tea. It was considered unfair as it had violated the right to be taxed only by own elected representatives as popularized by the slogan 'no taxation without representation'. Demonstrators threw tea chests into the sea, which came to be known as the Boston Tea Party, which ultimately escalated in the American Civil War. The same city in the late 20th century faced a massive problem of managing traffic. A huge project was conceived in the 1970s to connect the major places of the city—ports, city centres, airports, railway terminals, memorials, etc.

The planning started in the 1980s and construction work started in the 1990s and got completed in 2007. This project can be said to be one of the best, or worst, examples of how things can go awry with the passage of time, change in political leadership, induction of new technology and management principles and usage of poor quality material leading to time and cost overrun. The Big Dig has been one of the most expensive infrastructure projects in the USA, which involved a large number of private contractors, who had difference of opinions inter alia on the design, leading to various faulty designs being adopted, the use of material, administrative and political approvals, etc.

Huge sums had to be paid to individuals for restitution, and the project cost ballooned so much that it was nowhere connected to what had been envisaged and estimated in the beginning. When it was conceived in the 1970s, no one could have imagined even in the wildest of the dreams that the project would take such a long time to get completed and so much money would be sucked by the project. When the planning started in the early 1980s, there were serious environmental concerns, which were somehow allayed and efforts to receive the federal government funding started. The US Congress approved the funding; however, President Ronald Reagan found it to be too expensive and hence used his veto power. But the Congress was convinced and it overrode the president's veto.

This was a new beginning which brought chaos and confusion to the city of Boston, along with uncertainty, corrupt practices and the practice of cutting corners. Hardly anything was done on time and within the budget. The work started in the early 1990s; however, the state legislature of the state of Massachusetts created a separate legal entity to deal with the work. The Massachusetts Turnpike Authority (MTA) was constituted, which had no experience of handling a project of the magnitude of the Big Dig. So a JV was hired to do the work related to designs, construction, tracking, etc. Legally speaking, the MTA was independent of the hired JV, but employees from the two—MTA and the JV—started working together, making for all practical purposes, partners and, thus, creation of a PPP.

The engineering problems of making tunnels got escalated due to so many anticipated problems such as buried houses, sunken ships, underground pipelines and other existing tunnels; however, an interesting problem anticipated at that time was release of millions of rats on the streets of Boston by causing damage to their underground homes. It would have been a scene as visualized in 'The Pied Piper of Hamelin', and then waiting for the rodents to somehow follow the 'lemming suicidal tendency'. Engineering designs to take care of all such problems and environmental clearances from the local administration, state administration and also the federal government took a longish period of time and by then the inflation had taken its toll on the project cost.

With whatever delay the project had seen, there was a keen desire on the part of the political leadership—both in the state and in Washington—to get it finished as non-completion of this project would have been a big blot on a number of great minds who had put the project together. By the year 2004 and 2005, almost the entire project was completed and had been opened for public use. In 2006, two tunnels were dedicated to Thomas P. O'Neill Jr, the House of Representatives Speaker from Massachusetts who had been instrumental in securing funds for the project from the federal government.⁵³ According to certain estimates by the media, the total project had cost more than $20 billion and it would not have been possible at all—with all ups and downs in the project due to faulty design resulting in huge failures at times, which made tongue-lashing and blame-gaming routine—without the constant support of the political leadership.

CLOSED-CIRCUIT TELEVISION CAMERAS IN DELHI

Installation of closed-circuit television (CCTV) cameras, which are also called video surveillance cameras, has become almost an integral part of modern-day living, especially in urban areas. China is known for installing millions of such cameras all over the country to keep the activities of anyone on its soil under control and check. India, being a democratic country, can do the same only if it is permitted by the Constitutional and legal framework taking into account the privacy issues. The city of Delhi, which politically is a state in itself, has grown rapidly in the last couple of decades with crime rate going up exponentially, and the need to monitor the activities of the people in public areas has become urgent.

The democratically elected government of Delhi—Aam Aadmi Party (AAP), headed by the Chief Minister Arvind Kejriwal—had promised and decided to install a large number of CCTV in the city. Ideological differences between AAP and the ruling coalition at the centre, NDA, are well known with frequent clashes in the public between Kejriwal and the Prime Minister Narendra Modi. Delhi had been a union territory for a long period of time, which means it was being

---

⁵³ Andrew Miga, 'Politics Played Role in Boston's Big Dig,' *Star News Online*, 16 July 2006. Available at https://www.starnewsonline.com/news/20060716/politics-played-role-in-bostons-big-dig (accessed on 25 April 2019).

controlled and governed by the central government, and later on when it got statehood, indirect and subtle control of the central government on the city continued in the form of the position of lieutenant governor, who is supposed to be, de jure or de facto, a representative of the central government, though he's not supposed to be tilted towards either the central government or the state government; he is expected to be neutral and unbiased.

While AAP government in Delhi was planning to install the CCTVs, the lieutenant governor of Delhi formed a committee to regulate the installation and functioning of the surveillance cameras, with a member representing the central government included in the committee. This move was vehemently objected to by AAP government citing the reason that as it was a state activity, there was no need for any central representative to be a part of the overseeing committee. The lieutenant governor, however, was of the opinion that as New Delhi, being the capital of India, was extremely sensitive and important for the country as a whole and, therefore, it was fitting that the central government had also have a role in the governance of Delhi, at least in all the aspects related to security and privacy of the people.

Moreover, there has to be a concerted effort by the central and state governments in Delhi to make the city and the surrounding areas—known as the National Capital Region (NCR)—a better place to live and work in. The role of the committee was primarily to create the regulatory framework for the functioning of CCTV cameras and set up the standard operating procedure. The Delhi government had rejected the committee seeing it as a body without any legal basis and jurisdiction. It called the committee illegal and unconstitutional. The political tussle between the democratically elected government of Delhi and the lieutenant governor resulted in creation of unforeseen problems and situations like the chief minister of state sitting in protest against the decisions of the lieutenant governor.[54]

Creation of infrastructure, like the installation of CCTV cameras in the instant case, can be very painful, time-taking and uncertain political wrangling resulting in long legal battles, eventually leading to neglect of public interest and lots of opportunities. After almost three years of going back and forth, in January 2019, about 300 cameras were installed at select places in Delhi and the target is to have about 140,000 such cameras in 70 assembly constituencies, that is, 2,000 cameras in each constituency, by the time of completion of the scheme.[55] The project is under the supervision of the Public Works Department (PWD) of Delhi and not under the committee planned by the lieutenant governor. The number of cameras appears to be very high; however, given the very high profile of people living in Delhi and NCR, and the social and economic strata to which they belong, there has been a demand for a very long time for constant vigil to cut the rate of crime so as to make living in these areas safe and secure.

There is no doubt about it, but there is only one big question mark about the entire scheme—how to ensure that the scheme doesn't become a victim of change in political leadership and enforcement of new policies, as per the whims and fancies of

---

[54] TNN, 'Baijal Writes to Kejriwal on CCTV Project, CM Hits Back,' *The Times of India*, 14 May 2018. Available at https://timesofindia.indiatimes.com/city/delhi/baijal-writes-to-kejriwal-on-cctv-project-cm-hits-back/articleshow/64151789.cms (accessed on 25 April 2019).

[55] Alok K. N. Mishra and Pankhuri Yadav, 'AAP Govt's CCTV Plan Takes Off with 300 Cameras on Trial,' *The Times of India*, 15 January 2019. Available at https://timesofindia.indiatimes.com/city/delhi/aap-govts-cctv-plan-takes-off-with-300-cameras-on-trial/articleshow/67533943.cms (accessed on 25 April 2019).

the new political masters. This is one of the biggest challenges faced by infrastructure projects in democratic countries, and the legal route has not been found to be the most effective for public welfare.

NICE AND BMIC

Politicians have the uncanny ability to spring a surprise any time. Former Prime Minister of India, H. D. Deve Gowda, did the same in 2018 when he again picked up the issue of BMIC[56] which he had abandoned just two years back.[57] A little bit of history on this will be helpful to understand the political connection. Immediately after economic liberalization in 1991, it was felt that Bangalore, the capital city of the state of Karnataka, would see tremendous industrial growth and boom in information technology (IT) sector. Expansion of the city would be possible only to a certain limit and the old historic city of Mysore, with rich culture, heritage and business possibilities, was just 100 miles or about 150 km away.

The political leadership at that time decided that it would be a fantastic idea to connect the two cities with an expressway and for this purpose a MoU was signed by the State of Karnataka and a consortium of private companies in the presence of the then Chief Minister of Karnataka, Deve Gowda, and the governor of the American State of Massachusetts, whose presence was significant as a positive signal to the world about

---

[56] TNN, 'Deve Gowda: Will Take Action on NICE Report,' *The Times of India*, 24 November 2018. Available at https://timesofindia.indiatimes.com/city/bengaluru/deve-gowda-will-take-action-on-nice-report/articleshow/66779953.cms (accessed on 25 April 2019).

[57] TNN, 'Gowda Loses Hope, Ends 12-Year Fight against BMIC,' *The Times of India*, 17 August 2016. Available at https://timesofindia.indiatimes.com/city/bengaluru/Gowda-loses-hope-ends-12-year-fight-against-BMIC/articleshow/53730173.cms (accessed on 25 April 2019).

the confidence American government and businesses had in the Indian partners, the government of Karnataka and the growth potential of both the cities, Bangalore and Mysore. The private companies—Vanasse Hangen Brustlin, Inc. (VHB) USA; Kalyani Group of Companies, India; and SAB Engineering and Construction Inc. CSA—had formed the consortium. The project was thus planned on the PPP model.

The consortium created a corporate vehicle—NICE—for the implementation of the project. As luck would have it, Deve Gowda was appointed as the prime minister of India in June 1996 and remained in power for less than a year till April 1997. How could this happen is still a mystery. The simple explanation given by political commentators tells us that at that time among all the prime ministerial candidates, he had faced the least opposition and was thus acceptable to most of them. To clarify at this juncture, he did not become the prime minister due to his immense popularity or great public appeal. He was not even known as the national political leader as his main body of work was limited to the state of Karnataka.

For most of the prime ministerial aspirants, he was seen as the least troublesome and as someone who would keep the PM's seat warm for a short period of time, which would have given them the opportunity to go backstage and get going into certain political manoeuvrings. His short spell as the prime minister of India is not really worth remembering for anything of great national importance, except a national policy for agriculture, as he called himself the 'humble farmer'. Becoming the prime minister was the turning point and must have been one of the important reasons for bringing so many problems to the BMIC project.

After having served as the prime minister of the country, it was definitely infra dig for Deve Gowda to aspire to become the chief minister of the state of Karnataka and, unfortunately for him, he could not get enough support to again become the prime minister or a leader of national importance and, hence, he simply was spending time in Delhi and Bangalore looking for some political issue to connect with his people, though he must have had something clear in his mind that for all practical purposes his political career was over.

In the meantime, in November 1997, a public interest writ petition (PIL) was filed in the Karnataka High Court challenging the project inter alia on the ground that much more than necessary and adequate area of land was acquired to give benefit to the private entity NICE and the consortium, along with benefits to the key functionaries in the government, bureaucrats, technocrats, and anyone and everyone who was holding a position of power and influence. The state government and the NICE opposed the petition vehemently and averred that everything had been done according to the procedure established by law. The high court decided in favour of the State and the NICE and also observed that as it was a policy decision, it would not have been proper for the court to interfere in the matter. It was challenged in the Supreme Court, where also it had failed. Land acquisition was challenged by individual landowners in separate petitions and fresh PILs were filed against the project.

Surprisingly, the state government, which was till the other day supporting the NICE, changed its stand, started voicing the concerns of landowners and opposed the NICE. In 2004, there was a change in the government in Karnataka and Deve Gowda's son, H. D. Revanna, became the minister of the PWD. Gowda made serious allegations that the NICE was just a façade for acquiring land, and the NICE was factually in the real estate business. Revanna, due to his position as the PWD minister, got the project almost stalled. Everything slowed down from the government's side. Committees, lobbying, petitions, protests, political shadow-boxing, demonstrations, etc., became routine. Too many petitions of all kinds (PILs, land acquisition litigation, environment petitions, commercial cases, suits for recovery, bank recovery proceedings, etc.) were filed by different aggrieved parties.

The matter kept lingering on, and the people of Karnataka had almost given up the hope to get the NICE Road. Almost all the petitions, after undertaking the long and arduous legal journey, ended up in the Supreme Court—a good number of them could not manage to reach the Supreme Court due to some legal technicality, or the parties did not consider them worthy of being stretched that far—and in the 2006 judgement, the Supreme Court upheld the land acquisition and allowed the continuance of the project.[58] Despite the Supreme Court's decision, politicking kept its pace up and again several matters were filed, or were already pending, in different courts. No weapon in the armoury was left unused.

In a case being heard by a Supreme Court bench, Gowda's counsel—Shanti Bhushan, a very senior lawyer who had been the law minister of India from 1977 to 1979—stated that his client did not have faith in one of the judges on the bench,

---

[58] *State of Karnataka and Another v. All India Manufacturers Organisation and Others*; Supreme Court of India; 20 April 2006; Bench: B. N. Srikrishna, Ruma Pal, Dalveer Bhandari, JJ.; Reported in 2006 Indlaw SC 554; (2006) 4 SCC 683; AIR 2006 SC 1846; JT 2006 (11) SC 337; 2006 (4) KarLJ 369; 2006 (2) RCR(Civil) 596; 2006(4) SCALE 398; [2006] Suppl S.C.R. 86; Appeal (civil) 3492–3494 of 2005 with C.A. Nos. 3497/05, 3842–3844/05, 3848–3884/05, 3889–4127/05, 4128–4366/05, 4575–4576/05, 5399–5401/05, 5402/05, 5746–5747/05, 5759/05, 5797–5799/05, 6098/05, 6099/05, 5092–5093/05, 7024–7040/05, 7591/05, 7592/05, 61/06, 73/06, 74–76/06 and C.A. Nos./06 @ S.L.P. Nos. 1562–63/06.

Justice Arijit Pasayat, and hence prayed for his recusal. In the application, he wrote the reason as, 'reasonable apprehension regarding likelihood of bias and want of impartiality on the basis of the relevant material in his (Gowda's) possession'.[59] Justice Pasayat was shocked but he recused himself from the case. Political machinations have no limits. Gowda wanted to stall the project at any cost, and he had got some booklets printed making corruption charges against high and mighty in the NICE case, with the main blame being on the NICE itself.

Justice Pasayat had disapproved of the practice of anyone writing letters to judges on pending matters, and using this as an excuse, Gowda's counsel stated that the judge might have been biased against Gowda.[60] Strange argument indeed, but it was effective in the sense that the judge had recused and Gowda at least got some more time. Several criminal complaints were also filed in the matter alleging illegalities, irregularities and fraud in contract formation and other activities of NICE road project. These complaints were challenged by the NICE in the Karnataka High Court, which did not find any merit in the complaints and the court decided the case in NICE's favour.[61]

Political battle is still going on, and Deve Gowda has picked it up again in November 2018. To placate the voters in his constituency, and the state in general, Gowda identified a

---

[59] *Hindustan Times*, 'SC Judge Recuses from Hearing BMIC Issue on Deve Gowda's Plea,' 9 February 2009. Available at https://www.hindustantimes.com/india/sc-judge-recuses-from-hearing-bmic-issue-on-deve-gowda-s-plea/story-85BvtBIi88f3IRximGimyK.html (accessed on 25 April 2019).

[60] Samanwaya Rautray, 'Gowda Bias Slur Eases Out Judge,' *The Telegraph*, 10 February 2009. Available at https://www.telegraphindia.com/india/gowda-bias-slur-eases-out-judge/cid/499465 (accessed on 25 April 2019).

[61] *Nandi Infrastructure Corridor Enterprise Limited and others v. State by Lokayuktha Police, Bangalore and another;* Karnataka High Court; 27 June 2013; W.P. Nos. 45085–45086 of 2012 (GM-RES) Connected With W.P. No. 45151 of 2012 (GM-RES); Bench: Anand Byrareddy, J.; Reported 2013 Indlaw KAR 1775.

certain group of people who have been really troubled by the growth of the NICE road. Though it has been helpful in connecting places and providing better road access, the land acquired by the government, and thereafter given to a private developer, has been beyond the reasonable limits experienced in such road projects. Gowda has made accusations, time and again, that land is being used for developing private buildings, rather than for the benefit of the masses as what was envisaged. Of late, political instability in Karnataka has been one of the major factors which provided an opportunity to critics of the project—like Gowda himself—to sing the same tune of corruption in illegalities in the project.

However, the fact of the matter is that investors and business leaders have found the project to be good and truly beneficial to them and also to the society in the long run. Hence, for them it doesn't make sense to move out of the project, which is currently in advanced stage, and invest somewhere else. However, there are numerous unscrupulous business persons who have set up apparently small-time real estate businesses all along the BMIC and are befooling naïve and innocent persons into buying plots of land or apartments, for which they have no approval at all. Most of these so-called property dealers are closely connected to local political leaders and flourish in the business of property with their blessings. Property and politics go hand in hand.

BENGALURU–MYSURU EXPRESSWAY: NEW DEVELOPMENTS

While all the troubles with the NICE project have been going on the city of Mysore has suffered because of poor connectivity with Bangalore, which ought to have been taken care of and very well connected with proper completion of the NICE road. With very high demand for good connectivity, the government of Karnataka along with the NHAI planned to widen the existing four-lane road to six-lane road and for this purpose the contract was awarded to a Bhopal-based company Dilip Buildcon. The project is worth about $1 billion and has been divided into two parts to make the project feasible and manageable, both for the government and the private contract.[62] As there had been very serious political interventions on anything being constructed between these two cities, the government has been extremely cautious to attract new investors.

Uncertainties about undue political interference had practically miffed off the private parties and investors; however, the need of the people to have a proper Expressway between the two cities which can reduce the travel time to roughly 90 minutes had been the major driving force which somehow assured private parties of regular financial returns from the long-term project. It is encouraging to note that despite so many problems associated with the new roads connecting these two cities, there are private builders who are willing to take the risk and even fund the project on the basis of HAM, which is otherwise not the preferred model with the private companies when compared with EPC projects. We have discussed this earlier in the book while discussing the financial aspects of infrastructure projects and PPP.

The project being executed by the company Dilip Buildcon has, however, faced two major problems: environmental

---

[62] K. R. Balasubramanyam, 'Bhopal-Based Dilip Buildcon Wins Bengaluru–Mysuru E-Way Project,' *The Economic Times*, 1 March 2018. Available at https://economictimes.indiatimes.com/industry/indl-goods/svs/construction/bhopal-based-dilip-buildcon-wins-bengaluru-mysuru-e-way-project/articleshow/63121201.cms (accessed on 25 April 2019).

clearance and land acquisition.⁶³ Both these problems are related to local politics and some heavyweight politicians have been grinding their axes while the people and industry have suffered. It is quite obvious and natural for local politicians to show their compassion to the vulnerable sections of society in those geographical areas through which the road passes. The activity of construction of a road eventually results in losers and gainers—some people lose as their prime land is acquired and they do not get adequate compensation, and some people gain as they are able to dispose of their land, which otherwise was not saleable, at a very high price due to close proximity to the Expressway.

Local political leaders are able to influence the sections of the people and try to get the best political mileage according to the ground reality. This is truly political acumen and political jugglery, which is not possible for the common man who works hard to make both ends meet. As a substantial portion of the Expressway passes through the forest, the same old issue of 'environment versus development' needs to be handled in a practical manner keeping in mind the priority given to public interest, public purpose and benefit to the public at large. A good portion of the land needed for construction of the Expressway had been acquired long ago by the NICE project and is lying either unused or being used for certain purposes and not approved in the project.

Most of these portions of land have been de-notified and awarded to Dilip Buildcon on paper; however, getting physical possession has proved to be tricky. The going may not be

---

[63] S. Lalitha, 'Bengaluru–Mysuru Six Lane Project Faces Further Delay,' *The New Indian Express*, 22 September 2018. Available at http://www.newindianexpress.com/cities/bengaluru/2018/sep/22/bengaluru-mysuru-six-lane-project-faces-further-delay-1875529.html (accessed on 25 April 2019).

very smooth, but still the private company and the government have high hopes for the primary reason that the public requires this connectivity and it is all financially viable in the long run due to the presence of very heavy traffic even at the present time.

It is going to be challenging to get this project completed properly and within a reasonable period of time as political disposition will undoubtedly have its role in getting the clearances and quick movement of files within the government departments with proper alignment of the thought process, singularity of purpose and sense of urgency. Getting project funding from financial institutions and public sector banks can also be expedited and made easy with the help of proper political networking. Getting things not obstructed on any file due to certain flimsy grounds is also ensured by getting bureaucratic support and blessings of political masters. Newer political aspirations of families in politics—hopeful to have dynastic rule—are damaging for the public as rent seekers get well established in the system and suck it like a parasite. Meritocracy suffers and families in power get patronized.

LAND PORTS AUTHORITY OF INDIA: KARTARPUR SAHIB CORRIDOR

At the border with Pakistan, a corridor will be constructed which will connect the final resting place of Guru Nanak Dev—Darbar Sahib in Kartarpur Pakistan—with the Dera Baba Nanak shrine in Gurdaspur, Punjab, India. This has been approved by the political leaders of India and Pakistan, and will be constructed and operated by the Land Ports Authority of India (LPAI).[64] There is an urgency to complete

---

[64] http://www.lpai.gov.in/content/ (accessed on 25 April 2019).

the project by November 2019 to commemorate the 550th birth anniversary of Guru Nanak. The LPAI shall maintain the check posts and develop the terminal building for the pilgrims. There is also a plan to have a very high—about 100 m—Indian flag hoisted on the Indian side at the international border.[65] Approvals and clearances are being expedited by the central government to get the project completed in time.

This project is one of the best examples of political will and intention which can get done very complex—diplomatically and strategically—projects in the shortest possible time. If the technology needed is not proprietary and geographically no serious challenges are posed, a project gets slowed down either due to lack of funds or want of timely administrative decision-making. India has been trying to stand strong, confident and non-apologetic to Pakistan for a long time and for various reasons. The Kartarpur Sahib Corridor is a very good opportunity to exhibit India's strength, confidence and conviction. With land, money and approvals almost guaranteed, there is hardly any obstacle in the path and the LPAI is expected to do a good job by making this terminal truly magnificent, grand and functioning well.

The LPAI has been established in 2012 under the Land Ports Authority of India Act, 2010. One of the primary purposes of creating the LPAI is to have proper facilities for movement of people and goods across the international borders of India. The very long international land border—more than 15,000 km—India shares with its neighbours—China, Pakistan,

---

[65] *Hindustan Times*, '₹190 Crore Terminal on Anvil for Kartarpur Corridor,' 10 March 2019. Available at https://www.hindustantimes.com/chandigarh/rs-190-crore-terminal-on-anvil-for-kartarpur-corridor/story-bsNJhUelzpx96wOVs5A0hN.html (accessed on 25 April 2019).

Nepal, Bangladesh, Bhutan, Myanmar, Afghanistan—has its unique problems and challenges. Entry and exit points have to be closely monitored so that only legally permitted movements of people and goods take place. Traditional and old style methods are not at all effective in keeping a complete check on unlawful activities. Moreover, the genuine passengers and goods carriers often face inconvenience and avoidable harassment due to lack of proper facilities.

To streamline this process, integrated check posts (ICPs) are being constructed, something akin to what is experienced at airports and seaports.[66] These shall be really integrated with almost all the core and necessary sovereign functions—security, immigration, customs, quarantine, etc.—being performed at one place. Also, the support functions—parking, banking, warehousing, foreign exchange, etc.—shall be available. Other facilities will also be made available such as hotels, public conveniences, health services, refreshment outlets, telephone, post office and residential accommodation for the ICP staff. It is a very optimistic plan and the country needs to upgrade the existing set-up, which is bare minimum in most of the cases. There is also the requirement to have proper 'last mile connectivity' so that the ICPs are properly connected with road, or rail, or both with the nearest town or city.

A good way of doing it is with the help of dedicated bus service, and in case there is very high traffic, rail connectivity can also be planned. In any case, the ICPs should not be without any convenient, safe and affordable transfer facility. Ancillary buildings have to be constructed for this purpose. All this work can be easily done through the PPP model. Given the sensitive nature of the ICPs, too much private

---

[66] http://www.lpai.gov.in/content/innerpage/our-role.php (accessed on 25 April 2019).

participation cannot be encouraged; however, simple and plain construction work can be allotted to private parties with specifications to be complied with strictly. The LPAI Act clearly forbids private participation in any of the sovereign functions. No such function can be assigned to any private entity. For instance, the Attari–Wagah ICP is about 30 km from Amritsar and almost midway between Amritsar in India and Lahore in Pakistan.[67] At this ICP, movement of passengers and goods is monitored and facilitated.

These ICPs are very sensitive and the highest levels of security are maintained. Private participation in any of its functions, though commercially desirable, is not encouraged. Being highly strategic locations, control of the government of the day through political masters is almost absolute; however, professional decisions are taken by the experts trained in their respective domains. It is expected that political leadership will not unnecessarily interfere in the day-to-day functioning. Only major policy decisions are to be taken by the political masters that ensure a subtle control by the democratic processes.

KEY TAKEAWAYS

- *Political patronage:* Successful completion of PPP infrastructure projects, typically high value projects, require continuous political patronage at all the stages of the project. This patronage is needed irrespective of the party or coalition in power as in democratic countries, like India, the term of PPP projects may see several changes in the government. Hence, abiding interest in the project, rather than working on the whims and fancies of a

---

[67] http://www.lpai.gov.in/content/innerpage/icp-attari.php (accessed on 25 April 2019).

political leader in a position of power, helps in the long run. The fundamentals of any such PPP project should be so strong that any political leader—irrespective of party or coalition—finds it convincing and capable of making people happy. Any such project is bound to get political patronage.

- *Bureaucratic backing:* The steel frame of the country—the bureaucracy—is responsible for evaluating projects, setting norms and standards, making rules and regulations, inviting bids, processing them, deliberating on them in several committees, reporting to the political leaders and, thereafter, monitoring the progress of projects after award of contracts. The bureaucrats control numerous approvals, grants, allocation of funds, etc. They are generally intelligent, sharp and have an eye for details. It is always beneficial for any PPP project to have unflinching backing of the strong body of civil servants, which is possible by following the rule book strictly. Any deviation may result in administrative delay and judicial proceedings.

- *Public demand:* The real test of a PPP project is to understand the needs and demands of public. These usually vary from place to place, and time to time. As PPP projects are for a long duration of time, it is of utmost importance that the future needs and demands are properly anticipated, analysing whatever data can be collected. Assumptions made while doing this exercise should not be too simplistic, or far away from reality, otherwise the entire project may go out of sync with the real conditions and then fail drastically. Making realistic predictions is the key of a successful PPP project.

APPENDIX

IMPORTANT TERMS RELATED TO INFRASTRUCTURE PROJECTS

Arbitral tribunal: The group of arbitrators resolving a dispute. It may have a single (sole) arbitrator, or more than one, usually in odd number. Most common being with one or three arbitrators.

Arbitration: A private forum for resolution of disputes, typically with neutral experts chosen mutually by disputants.

Arbitrator: Member of an arbitral tribunal chosen mutually by the disputing parties.

Award: The decision of an arbitral tribunal. It can be challenged in a court of law on specific and narrow grounds as provided in the arbitration law applicable in a particular jurisdiction.

Bid: A proposal or offer made by a bidder.

Bidder: A party which submits a bid in response to an EOI, or an invitation to submit a bid.

Bidding: The process of submitting a bid by a bidder.

BOLT: Build–own–lease–transfer

BOOT: Build–own–operate–transfer. The concessionaire builds, owns, operates a project and, at the completion of the concession period, hands it over to the sponsoring public authority, which has awarded the concession. This PPP model is typically used for real estate projects.

BOT: Build–operate–transfer. The concessionaire builds, operates and transfers the project at the end of the concession to the sponsoring public authority. This PPP model is typically used for road projects.

Brownfield project: Project on a site where some infrastructure assets were in existence, or have been used for industrial purpose, etc. It is contradistinguished with a greenfield project.

COD: Commercial operations date. This is the date when the commercial operations start in a PPP project after the end of construction.

Concession: Concession is the grant of certain rights in a public asset by the government or a public authority to a private party. In PPP, it usually comes with important economic rights to exploit that public asset commercially for a certain period of time which is the term of CA. Most of the revenue in a concession comes from the public users.

CA: The contract for concession between a government body and a concessionaire is known as a CA. It is the grant of those concession rights to a private entity which are otherwise vested with the government body. The same is true for CAs for public service, which usually are undertaken by a government body.

Concessionaire: Concessionaire is the private party to a CA. It can be a single company or a consortium of companies.

DB: Design–build

DBF: Design–build–finance

DBFM: Design–build–finance–maintain

DBFO: Design–build–finance–operate

DBFOM: Design–build–finance–operate–maintain

DBFOT: Design–build–finance–operate–transfer

DBO: Design–build–operate. The government body arranges funding.

EOI: The very first stage of the bidding process to gauge the interest of parties to go ahead with the issuance of technical and financial qualifications, and thereafter shortlisting for bids. The primary purpose is to filter out serious players. Many a time used interchangeably with RfQ.

EPC: Engineering, procurement and construction. This has been the most common model of getting public work done by private contractors. With the PPPs becoming popular, the private contractor is supposed to take a bigger role in the projects by arranging finance, operating, maintaining, collecting revenue, etc. EPC involved all the steps from the initial stage till the completion stage of a project—designing, engineering, procuring material and equipment (material might be provided by the government body), constructing, etc. These were typically turnkey projects with fixed price and a scheduled completion date.

Expropriation: The State takes over a private company or project in public interest. Compensation to the private party is generally paid.

FIDIC: Fédération Internationale Des Ingénieurs-Conseils. International Federation of Consulting Engineers. FIDIC standard contract conditions are used globally for construction projects with necessary modifications, if required.

Fixed price contract: The contractor takes the maximum risk. He has the full responsibility of delivering at the price fixed in the contract, without any flexibility. No change is possible.

Force majeure: Situations beyond one's control, either due to natural forces—act of God—or man-made.

Greenfield project: Project at a site where there had been no industry or significant infrastructure.

L1: The lowest financial bid. Has important implications in award of public contracts.

LoA: Letter of acceptance. The letter awarding the contract to the selected bidder after evaluation of all bids and final selection.

LoC: Letter of credit. Typically a bank guarantee given in writing by a bank to a beneficiary at the instructions of an applicant. LoC guarantees payment to the beneficiary by the bank on presenting some pre-decided documents.

LoI: Letter of intent. An understanding between two parties in the form of a document. It may be binding or non-binding in a court of law, according to the context. Usually parties coming together in a consortium sign a letter of intent, and it is generally a binding legal document.

MCA: Standard CAs prepared by government authorities as a basic framework for different infrastructure sectors. These can be modified according to the needs and requirements of the parties.

Negotiation: Discussion or dialogue between the parties, usually at the pre-bid stage to clarify any doubts or to express genuine concerns to get the terms of the tender modified. Negotiation can also be done to resolve any contractual or other differences at any stage of the project. The parties must convince each other to arrive at a satisfactory and acceptable solution.

Pre-bid meeting: Meeting with shortlisted bidders to clarify any doubts before receiving formal proposals.

Preferred bidder: The shortlisted bidder with whom the government authority negotiates for mutual benefit.

Pre-qualification: The first stage of a public procurement process.

Public goods: Infrastructure freely available to the public, and for which they can't be charged.

RfP: Only financial proposals are invited from the bidders shortlisted after the first stage—technical qualifications stage—in a two-stage bidding process, which necessarily involves qualifications and financial bids.

RfQ: Many a time used interchangeably with EOI. For inviting potential bidders to submit their first bid in a two-stage bidding. Only technically and financially qualified bidders are shortlisted for the next stage of submitting the financial bid.

Single-stage bidding: Contradistinguished with two-stage bidding. Used for small value projects. Technical and financial bids are invited simultaneously from the bidders.

Sunk costs: Fixed costs, also called upfront costs, incurred in the beginning of a project.

Swiss challenge: Unsolicited proposal made by a private entity to a public authority for some project, the proposer understands is in public interest. Open bidding is done and if some other entity makes a lower financial bid, though technically at par, the original proposer can match it and get the contract. It is not favoured much in India.

Turnkey projects: Usually EPC contract with the contractor taking complete responsibility for design, engineering, procurement, construction, etc.

Two-stage bidding: Contradistinguished with single-stage bidding. Used for large and high value projects. First, technical bids are invited along with documents to ensure financial capability to undertake large projects, and only those bidders who qualify are invited to submit their financial bids.

Unsolicited proposal: A private party submits a proposal without any notice inviting EOI, or tender, or any other invitation. This is the starting point in a Swiss challenge method.

Yellowfield project: Project in between brownfield and greenfield with some existing industry or infrastructure.

ABOUT THE AUTHOR

A Harvard Law School graduate, Anurag K. Agarwal has been the first recipient of the prestigious Marti Mannariah Gurunath Outstanding Teacher Award at the Indian Institute of Management Ahmedabad (IIMA). As faculty at IIMA, his teaching, consulting and research interests include business leadership, negotiation, strategy and law, infrastructure and PPPs, contracts and arbitration, intellectual property and related issues.

Graduated as Mechanical Engineer in 1990 from Motilal Nehru Regional Engineering College, Allahabad—now known as Motilal Nehru National Institute of Technology—he started his career with Bharat Petroleum Corporation Limited, where he worked for less than a year. Thereafter, he studied law at the Lucknow University, where he completed bachelor of laws (LLB)—gold medallist at the college—master of laws (LLM)—gold medallist at the University and doctor of laws (LLD). He went to Harvard Law School for a second master of laws (LLM). He was a practising lawyer in Lucknow and Delhi for nine years. He switched over to full-time teaching in 2004, with a brief stint at Management Development Institute, Gurugram, and joined IIMA in October 2004.

He conducts classes for several executive education programmes for government, public sector and private sector companies. He is a visiting faculty at many educational institutions. He is also on the board of some judicial, government and educational bodies.

He has authored five books: *Legal Language and Business Communication* (2019), *Business Law for Managers: Kaleidoscopic Tales* (2018), *Business Leadership and Law* (2017), *Contracts and Arbitration for Managers* (2016), and *Business and Intellectual Property* (2010). He writes a weekly column 'Lawfully Yours' for *DNA* Ahmedabad.

In this wonderful book, R. Anand provides practical advice that can help you make the most of your life. Anand combines ancient wisdom and modern science, storytelling and compelling data, all in the service of helping you find more happiness as well as more success.

Tal Ben-Shahar
Author of Happier

Finding happiness and well-being at work through mindfulness.

For special offers on this and other books from SAGE, write to
marketing@sagepub.in

Explore our range at
www.sagepub.in

Paperback
978-93-528-0805-2